Applications Workbook

Procedures & Theory
for Administrative Professionals

SIXTH EDITION

Patsy Fulton-Calkins, Ph. D.
Director of the Bill J. Priest Center
University of North Texas
Denton, TX

Karin M. Stulz, M.A.E.
Assistant Professor
Northern Michigan University
Marquette, MI

SOUTH-WESTERN
CENGAGE Learning

Australia • Brazil • Japan • Korea • Mexico • Singapore • Spain • United Kingdom • United States

SOUTH-WESTERN
CENGAGE Learning

Workbook to Accompany Procedures & Theory for Administrative Professionals, 6e

Dr. Patsy Fulton-Calkins and Karin M. Stulz

VP/Editorial Director: Jack W. Calhoun

VP/Editor-in-Chief: Karen Schmohe

Acquisitions Editor: Jane Phelan

Senior Developmental Editor: Dave Lafferty

Consulting Editor: Dianne Rankin

Editorial Assistant: Connor Allen

Senior Marketing Communications Manager: Terron Sanders

Marketing Manager: Valarie Lauer

Marketing Coordinator: Kelley Gilreath

Production Manager: Patricia Boies

Content Project Manager: Corey Geissler

Senior Technology Project Manager: Mike Jackson

Production Technology Analyst: Erin Donohoe

Manufacturing Coordinator: Kevin Kluck

Art Director: Bethany Casey

Internal Designer: c miller design

Cover Designer: c miller design

Cover Image: © GettyImages, Inc.

Photography Manager: Deanna Ettinger

Production Service: Pre-PressPMG

© 2008 Cengage Learning. All Rights Reserved.

ISBN-13: 978-0-538-73053-2
ISBN-10: 0-538-73053-6

South-Western Cengage Learning
5191 Natorp Boulevard
Mason, OH 45040
USA

Cengage Learning products are represented in Canada by Nelson Education, Ltd.

For your course and learning solutions, visit **school.cengage.com**

Procedures & Theory for Administrative Professionals, 6e
Copyright Notices

Printed in the United States of America
1 2 3 4 5 6 7 11 10 09 08

CONTENTS

Chapter 1   The Workplace—Constantly Changing

What's the Problem?

YOUR ORGANIZATION

You attend college full-time and work 16 hours each week for United Pharmaceuticals. United's home location is in Fort Worth, Texas. You are a part-time assistant to two administrative assistants, Melody Hoover and Amando Hinojosa, who report to Teresa Winwright, vice president of marketing. You report directly to Melody and Amando; they have asked that you address them by their first names. You take classes each morning; you are presently enrolled in 12 hours. You work at United Pharmaceuticals from
1 p.m. to 5 p.m. four days per week. You do not work on Fridays.

United Pharmaceuticals researches and markets the products it produces. In addition to its main office in Texas, it has locations in Los Angeles, California; New York, New York; Grand Rapids, Michigan; China; and India. Its main interests at the present time are cancer and stem cell research. In addition to research, United Pharmaceuticals markets a broad range of medicines throughout the world. Since the company's inception ten years ago, it has grown significantly and now sells more than $25 million dollars of products worldwide each year.

United Pharmaceuticals has a 15-member board of directors composed of men and women from major corporations within the United States, China, and India. It has three board meetings each year, with one held at the main office in Fort Worth, Texas. The other two are accomplished through Web conferencing so that the board members only need to travel to the home office once each year. The CEO of United Pharmaceuticals is David Anderson, Ph.D.

Mail and email addresses of the CEO and vice presidents of marketing in the United States and email addresses for presidents and vice presidents of the two international locations are as follows:

David Anderson, Ph.D., CEO
United Pharmaceuticals
1211 East Eighth Street
Fort Worth, TX 76102-5201
Email: DAnderson@up.com

Rene Gonzales
Vice President of Marketing
United Pharmaceuticals
205 Palm Street
Los Angeles, CA 93510-0205
Email: RGonzales@la.com

Edwardo Sanchez
Vice President of Marketing
United Pharmaceuticals
12 Fifth Avenue
New York, NY 10027-0012
Email: ESanchez@ny.com

John Hamilton
Vice President of Marketing
United Pharmaceuticals
184 5th Street
Grand Rapids, MI 49504-0184
Email: JHamilton@gr.com

New Delhi, India
Sunil Vettickal, President
Email: Svettickal@new.com

Ahmed Dieppe, Vice President of Marketing
Email: Adieppe@new.com

Gungzhou, China
Yao Chen, President
Email: Ychen@gua.com

Danixa Li, Vice President of Marketing
Email: Dli@gua.com

MISSION

United Pharmaceuticals is committed to excellence in the research and production of life-saving products, both nationally and internationally. As a pharmaceutical leader in the United States and the world, we are dedicated to making a difference in the quality and breadth of medicines available to help care for the world's population.

OUR VALUES

We adhere to the following values in guiding our health care decisions:
- Our business is improving human life. As an organization, we are deeply committed to continual scientific research that provides health and wellness for people throughout the world.
- The highest ethical standards are upheld.
- In our work environment, all individuals are valued and treated with respect and dignity.
- Teamwork is essential in producing quality pharmaceutical research and products.
- Ethnic diversity and diversity of thought and action are essential to our success.
- Contributions to our communities and our environment are essential.
- Since productivity and profitability are important to our long-term success, consistent attention is given to both areas.

English and Word Usage Drill

DIRECTIONS: Review the abbreviation rules in the Reference Guide of your textbook. Then correct the sentences below. Some sentences may be correct as written. Cite the rule that applies.

1. Doctor Cindy Boswick will be presenting the program on ethics at our April meeting of IAAP.

   Rule

2. Reverend Jacob Mathias spoke at the evening service of Forest Hills Presbyterian Church.

   Rule

3. The concert will be at 3 p.m..

   Rule

4. The company is located at W. Apple Lane.

   Rule

5. The Hon. Eleanor Isenberg will speak at the commencement.

   Rule

6. AT&T has expanded its operations.

   Rule

7. We are scheduled to take a IQ test tomorrow.

   Rule

8. The game is scheduled to take place on Mar. 15.

   Rule

9. A large No. of people were at the party.

   Rule

10. Several companies are under investigation by the F.T.C.

    Rule

Review Job Openings

DIRECTIONS: Review the five job openings and the questions below. Respond to the questions in a memo to your instructor. Use the *Microsoft® Word* file *Memo Form* found on the Student CD to prepare the memo. Find one real, current job ad similar to one of the five provided below and attach it to the memo.

1. What required qualifications do the jobs have in common?

2. Which jobs require a specific period of work experience?

3. Which of the jobs listed seems to you to be the lowest level position? the highest level position?

4. Which jobs listed require qualifications that most closely match your current qualifications? What additional qualifications do you need to be prepared for those jobs?

ADMINISTRATIVE ASSISTANT

MMCC Corporation is looking for a full-time administrative assistant for its Dallas, Texas, facility.
Responsibilities:
Handling a switchboard for incoming and outgoing calls
Organizing, filing, and handling the daily office operations
Computer experience is required (*Microsoft Office, Outlook*®)

MMCC offers a full benefits package (medical, dental, and life insurance) and paid vacation. Please fax resume with cover letter to: Ms. Elma Cardova, Central District Service Manager (800-555-0156).

OFFICE ASSISTANT

Environment, Inc., a growing company, has an immediate opening for an office assistant. Responsibilities include resident relocations, answering the phones, and processing invoices and reports. Requires computer skills (*Microsoft Office*), excellent interpersonal and customer service skills, and organizational skills. Room for advancement. Mail your resume to: Environment, Inc., 4500 13th Street, Colleyville, TX 76034-4500.

EXECUTIVE ADMINISTRATIVE ASSISTANT

North Dallas-based oil company is seeking experienced executive administrative assistant with knowledge of *Word, Excel*®, and *PowerPoint*®. Good communication skills and ability to work independently are required. Fax resume to 214-555-0174.

ADMINISTRATIVE ASSISTANT

TCCC has an immediate opening for an administrative assistant in its Dallas office. This position requires an individual who can work independently, possesses excellent verbal and written communication skills, and thrives on multitasking and working in a fast-paced environment. Responsibilities include data entry, filing, faxing, emailing, overseeing mailings, and answering the phones. Working knowledge of *Microsoft Word, Excel*, and database programs a must. Qualified candidates submit resume by fax to 972-555-0130.

EXECUTIVE ADMINISTRATIVE ASSISTANT

An established company in Fort Worth is seeking an experienced executive administrative assistant. The ideal candidate will be a team player who has exceptional secretarial skills with five years of experience reporting to senior management levels. This is a highly visible position requiring a polished professional to meet and greet clients, customers, and visitors to the president's office and to interact with upper management. Excellent organizational skills as well as advanced computer skills in *Word*, *Excel*, and *PowerPoint* are necessary to prepare confidential correspondence, statistical reports, and presentation materials. Fax resume to 817-555-0102.

Review the IAAP Website

DIRECTIONS:

1. Access the Website for this textbook at academic.cengage.com/officetech/fulton-calkins. Access the Website of the IAAP, using the link provided on the Links page.

2. Preview the types of articles in the current issue of *OfficePro*® magazine.

3. Review some of the jobs that are available on OfficeTeam®.

4. Write a summary of your findings in a memo to your instructor. Use the *Word* file *Memo Form* found on the Student CD to prepare the memo.

Professional Growth Plan

DIRECTIONS:

1. Think about where you want to be five years from now in your professional life. Identify specific goals that you want to achieve. List these goals and include a completion date. Identify at least three goals that you plan to achieve this semester.

2. Make a list of all the skills that you think you have, such as keyboarding, computer (listing the various computer competencies that you have), human relations skills, and so forth. Be honest with yourself; do not list skills that you wish you had but do not at this point. Title the list "Skills that I Possess Presently."

3. Complete the self-evaluation chart on the following page. Discuss your evaluation with a trusted friend, coworker, or family member to see if the person agrees with your ratings. Keep your self-evaluation; you will rate yourself again at the end of the course to determine the areas in which you have improved.

4. Using the list of skills that you possess presently and the self-evaluation chart, determine areas of growth that you need to focus on in this course. Develop a list of growth objectives that you want to accomplish during this course. Title the list "Areas of Growth for (list semester and date)."

5. At the completion of this course, you will be asked if you met your growth objectives. Your instructor may want you to turn in both the initial list of goals and objectives and the final evaluation. Check with the instructor as to her/his wishes.

SELF-EVALUATION CHART

DIRECTIONS: These questions are intended to help you examine personality and character traits. In Column 1, answer each question with *yes*, *no*, or *sometimes*. Keep this chart; you will complete Column 2 near the end of this course.

	Column 1	Column 2
CONFIDENCE AND COURAGE		
Do you have confidence in your skills and abilities?		
Do you stand up for what you think is right?		
Do you continue to try in spite of failures?		
POISE		
Are you patient with others?		
Do you remain calm in stressful situations?		
INITIATIVE AND AMBITION		
Do you make decisions instead of relying on others?		
Do you do more than is expected of you?		
Do you make good use of your spare time?		
Do you take pride in doing good work?		
KNOWLEDGE AND JUDGMENT		
Do you like to learn new things?		
Do you ask questions about things you do not understand?		
Do you think before you act?		
DEPENDABILITY		
Are you punctual?		
Do you follow through on promises you make?		
Can you be counted on to get a job done?		
INTEGRITY		
Are you trustworthy?		
Do you respect the opinions of others?		
Are you faithful in performing what is expected of you?		
Do you value high moral and ethical standards?		
GETTING ALONG WITH OTHERS		
Do you listen attentively when someone is talking?		
Do you try to find something good in everyone?		
Are you cheerful?		
Do you avoid criticizing others?		
DETERMINATION AND PERSEVERANCE		
Do you stay with a job until it is finished?		
Are you discouraged easily?		
Do you willingly accept difficult assignments?		

Web Research

DIRECTIONS:

1. Search the Internet and other sources to find the following information:
   - The most recent population diversity statistics for your state
   - Projected population diversity statistics in your state or in the United States for the next ten years

2. Write a short unbound report to discuss your findings. Include at least one chart in the report to illustrate diversity statistics.

Assessment of Chapter Goals

DIRECTIONS: Review the Chapter 1 goals listed here. Did you successfully complete these goals? Evaluate yourself by completing the form below. If you did not satisfy the goal, state your reason(s) for not doing so.

1. Identify changes that are occurring in the workplace.

   Yes_____   No_____

2. Define common types of business organizational structures.

   Yes_____   No_____

3. Determine major challenges confronting both management and administrative professionals.

   Yes_____   No_____

4. Explain crucial skills and qualities for an administrative professional.

   Yes_____   No_____

5. Determine how an effective administrative professional sets goals and makes decisions.

   Yes_____   No_____

Chapter 2   Workplace Team and Environment

English and Word Usage Drill

DIRECTIONS: Review the Bias-Free Language usage section in the Reference Guide of your textbook. Then correct the sentences below in the space provided. Some sentences may be correct as written. Cite the rule that applies.

1. The policemen demonstrated bravery.

    Rule

2. Handicapped individuals were competing in a basketball tournament.

    Rule

3. A growing number of Orientals live in the United States.

    Rule

4. The administrative professional answered her phone.

    Rule

5. A number of Indians live on reservations.

    Rule

6. Each doctor should send a nurse to the workshop.

Rule

7. The chairman of the committee mailed the agenda on Monday.

Rule

8. The effect of smoking has been studied extensively in rats and man.

Rule

9. Justina and I went to the Latina social party last week.

Rule

10. Each student must meet with his professor.

Rule

2-3 Case Study: Workplace Diversity (Goal 2)

DIRECTIONS: Read the case below and respond to the questions. Submit your responses to your instructor in a memo. Use the *Word* file *Memo Form* provided on the Student CD.

CASE:

United Pharmaceuticals is committed to diversity in the workplace. Last month two job openings appeared in the newspaper for administrative assistants. Human resources received 50 applications for the two jobs. You are serving on a committee (composed of five administrative assistants) to select the top three candidates for each position. Skills mentioned in the newspaper ad include computer, filing, interpersonal, communication, and teamwork skills. Human Resources gave candidates the option of submitting a form that identifies their race/ethnicity. The committee members agree that they will go through the applications individually and select the six most qualified candidates. Then a team meeting will be held to come to a consensus on the top six candidates. The team will submit the names of the top six candidates to the Human Resources Department.

When you have your group meeting, you discover you are the only person who has selected candidates of racial/ethnic diversity. The criteria you used for selection includes the skills identified for the job by United Pharmaceuticals. You believe you have selected the most qualified candidates. As you defend your position to the group, three team members become agitated. These members tell you that the two candidates are not qualified for the job. The fourth team member is silent. The argument becomes heated, so the team agrees to come back for a second meeting after each member has spent additional time looking over the applications. At the conclusion of the initial meeting, the fourth team member comes to you and tells you she thinks you are right.

QUESTIONS:

1. What should you say to the fourth team member?

2. How should you handle the next team meeting?

3. If the three team members still refuse to accept the qualifications of your candidates, what should you do?

Memo Report on Lower Back Injuries

ABC Company has 300 workers in manufacturing jobs, 25 workers in warehouse jobs, and 20 workers in shipping jobs. Over the past three years, the company has noted an increase in the number of lower back injuries among these workers. The company conducted a pilot training program in an attempt to decrease the number of lower back injuries. Workers in the Shipping Department were given training on the proper way to lift heavy objects. They were also given supportive back belts to wear at work.

DIRECTIONS:

1. Using your spreadsheet software, find the percent of employees in each department that reported lower back injuries. Show one decimal place in the percents. Create a column chart to compare the percent of lower back injuries reported by each department last year. Title the chart "LOWER BACK INJURIES 20--" (Use last year for the year.)

Manufacturing Department	25 injuries
Warehouse Department	5 injuries
Shipping Department	5 injuries

2. Create another column chart to compare the percent of lower back injuries reported by each department this year after the Shipping Department completed the training program. Title the chart "LOWER BACK INJURIES 20--" (Use the current year for the year.)

Manufacturing Department	26 injuries
Warehouse Department	6 injuries
Shipping Department	2 injuries

3. Create a memo to Kim Park, Director of Human Resources, from you, using the *ABC Company Memo Form* file found on the Student CD. Use today's date and an appropriate subject line. In the memo, mention that a large number of lower back injuries have been reported in recent years and discuss the pilot training program that was conducted in an attempt to decrease lower back injuries. Include the two charts you created in the memo, introducing each one appropriately. Mention the percent by which the number of injuries in the Shipping Department has changed since the pilot program and the percent change in injuries in the other two departments that did not participate in the pilot training program. Recommend whether the company should conduct the training program with the other two departments, Manufacturing and Warehouse.

Research Cultural Differences in Communication

DIRECTIONS: In addition to their locations in the United Sates, United Pharmaceuticals has locations in China and India. Because of this, your supervisor and colleagues spend a great deal of time working and communicating with employees from these countries. Your supervisor has decided to create a handout to help new employees understand some of the cultural differences that exist when communicating. Choose one of the international locations of United Pharmaceuticals and research the following questions. Prepare a handout that your supervisor can share with new employees.

1. What is an appropriate verbal greeting?

2. What is an appropriate nonverbal greeting?

3. Are there societal topics that should not be discussed (religion, government, family)?

4. Are there specific words that may have a vulgar or slang connotation that are used regularly in your culture that should be avoided?

5. Are there nonverbal communications (body language, hand or facial gestures) that could inadvertently affect your message?

Working as a Team, NASA's Problems in Space

DIRECTIONS: Imagine that you are part of a space exploration mission flying from a space station orbiting the Moon to a base on the Moon itself. An instrument malfunction causes you to crash on the Moon on the daylight side about 120 kilometers from the base. Your spacecraft is in need of repair and your survival depends upon reaching the Moon base as soon as possible[1].

1. Of the 15 items which were not damaged in the crash of your spacecraft, which would be most important for the 120-kilometer trip? Rank the items from most important (#1) to least important (#15) using the form on the following page. Write your rankings in the Individual Ranking column.

2. Once you have completed your rankings, choose three or four classmates to work with on this project. As a group, rank each of the 15 items. You **must** reach a consensus on the rankings. Record your group rankings on the form.

3. When all groups have agreed upon their rankings, ask your instructor for the NASA rankings and record them on the form. For each item, mark the number of points that your group score differs from the NASA ranking, then add up all the points. Disregard plus or minus differences. The *lower* the total, the better your score.

   Scores
   0–25 excellent
   26–32 good
   33–45 average
   46–55 fair
   56–70 poor
   71–112 very poor

---

[1] "Problems in Space," accessed January 6, 2007, available from http://starchild.gsfc.nasa.gov/docs/StarChild/space_level2/activity/problems_space.html.

Individual Ranking	Item	Group Ranking	NASA Ranking	Difference
_____	Box of matches	_____	_____	_____
_____	Food concentrate	_____	_____	_____
_____	Eighteen meters of nylon rope	_____	_____	_____
_____	Parachute silk	_____	_____	_____
_____	Solar-powered heating unit	_____	_____	_____
_____	Two 0.45 caliber pistols	_____	_____	_____
_____	One case of powdered milk	_____	_____	_____
_____	Two tanks of oxygen	_____	_____	_____
_____	Stellar map (of the Moon's constellations)	_____	_____	_____
_____	Self-inflating life raft	_____	_____	_____
_____	Magnetic compass	_____	_____	_____
_____	Fifteen liters of water	_____	_____	_____
_____	Signal flares	_____	_____	_____
_____	First aid kit containing needles for vitamins, medicine, etc., which can be administered through an opening in the spacesuits	_____	_____	_____
_____	Solar-powered FM Walkie-Talkie	_____	_____	_____

Assessment of Chapter Goals

DIRECTIONS: Review the Chapter 2 goals listed here. Did you successfully complete these goals? Evaluate yourself by completing the form below. If you did not satisfy the goal, state your reason(s) for not doing so.

1. Develop an understanding of effective team behavior and workplace team composition.

   Yes_____   No_____

2. Demonstrate effectiveness in dealing with people from diverse backgrounds.

   Yes_____   No_____

3. Engage in productive team communication.

   Yes_____   No_____

4. Describe the role of safety and health in the workplace.

   Yes_____   No_____

Chapter 3   The Virtual Workforce

English and Word Usage Drill

DIRECTIONS: Review the Capitalization section in the Reference Guide of your textbook. Then correct the sentences below in the space provided. Some sentences may be correct as written. Cite the rule that applies.

1. Superior University is offering astronomy 205 and ethics 201 on Saturday mornings.

    Rule

2. The professor started the lecture by stating, "today we will discuss oral communication and listening skills."

    Rule

3. My parents moved from the east to the south before I was born.

    Rule

4. The president of the United States visited with the hurricane victims.

    Rule

5. The biggest fundraiser for the girl scouts is their annual cookie sale.

    Rule

6. This year Christmas will be on Tuesday.

    Rule

7. For our summer vacation, our family is traveling to michigan to take a tour around lake superior.

    Rule

8. The annual conference will be held at the Spangler Hotel on Fifth Avenue.

    Rule

9. I asked uncle Carlos and aunt Rosita when my cousins were going to visit.

    Rule

10. The guest speaker will be Professor Garcia from the School of Medicine.

    Rule

Case Study: Working as a Virtual Assistant

DIRECTIONS: Read the case below and consider the questions. Discuss the case with three of your classmates. As a group write a summary of your responses in a memo to your instructor. Use the *Word* file *Memo Form* found on the Student CD to prepare the memo.

CASE:

Robin has been working as a virtual assistant for three months. Prior to that time, Robin was working full time in an administrative professional position. Robin has two children aged two and four. She wanted to spend more time with her children, and she thought working as a virtual assistant would provide her with more family time. However, after one month, Robin is not certain she made the right choice in deciding to work at home.

Robin's husband Luke also works from home three days a week. On those days, Robin and her husband share childcare responsibilities. Her husband works from noon to 8 p.m. Robin works from 7 a.m. until noon and from 9 p.m. until midnight. Luke is responsible for the children from the time they wake up in the morning until noon. Robin is responsible for them from noon until 8 p.m. However, during the past two weeks, both children have been ill. As a result, Robin and Luke are stressed and tired.

Robin is still trying to locate clients. Although she has an excellent work record from her previous jobs, she is finding it hard to make contacts and get clients. Currently she has four clients, but she is finding that they are not providing her with enough work (and income). She is only working about four hours a day. She needs more work to make up for the income she gave up when she quit her job. Robin thinks she is getting her work done in a satisfactory manner most of the time. However, when the kids were sick, she missed a major deadline for one of her important clients. Although the client did not seem upset, she is afraid missing the deadline will impact the amount of work she gets from that client in the future.

Robin and Luke have no help with the housework, and they often argue about who does what. Robin and Luke share an office. Robin finds that Luke is not very good about putting office supplies back where they belong. He also often leaves his work stacked in piles around the desk, which she often has to move before she can begin her work. The office is located next to the children's room, and sometimes the noise is distracting to her.

Robin also feels very isolated. She misses the daily contact she had with her coworkers. She misses working with colleagues on projects. Although she quit her job to spend more time with her family, she is finding that she now sees less of her husband. Also, most of the time she spends with her children is by herself while her husband is working.

QUESTIONS:

1. What are the major issues facing Robin and Luke?

2. Should Robin consider going back to the traditional workplace? If so, will this create other issues for Robin?

3. What suggestions do you have for Robin if she continues working as a virtual assistant?

Telecommuting Personal Screener

DIRECTIONS: Rate yourself on each of the factors listed in the Telecommuting Personal Screener. (H=high M=medium L=low)

The U.S. Department of Housing and Urban Development uses the following screener to help employees determine their current readiness to be a successful teleworker. This tool is organized in three parts: Prerequisites, Skills, and Work Style. This screener will help you identify your strengths, as well as barriers that you may need to overcome.[1]

TELECOMMUTING PERSONAL SCREENER

Prerequisites

Every successful telecommuter must have job knowledge and experience that can enable him/her to work independently. These factors are part of the following set of prerequisites.

		Circle One		
1.	Level of job knowledge	H	M	L
2	Amount of job experience	H	M	L
3.	Productivity	H	M	L
4.	Overall quality of work	H	M	L
5.	Adaptability of current job to the non-traditional work setting/operation	H	M	L
6.	Ability to adapt home environment to an office-like environment	H	M	L

---

[1] "Telecommuting Personal Screener," U.S. Department of Housing and Urban Development, accessed February 22, 2007, available from http://www.hud.gov/offices/adm/jobs/telework/telwork7.cfm.

Skills

Below are types of skills required for telecommuting success. Consider how you rate in each listed skill group and circle the appropriate rating on a scale from high to low.

		Circle One	
1. Organizational and planning skills	H	M	L
2. Project management skills	H	M	L
3. Time management skills/ability to structure time in an unstructured environment	H	M	L
4. Self-discipline/ability to manage potential conflict between personal and work commitments	H	M	L
5. Communication skills: oral	H	M	L
6. Communication skills: written	H	M	L
7. Technology literacy level/ability to work	H	M	L

Work Style

Think about how your work style or personality is suited to working away from a traditional office environment. Your work environment will be much less structured and supervision, coaching, and feedback will likely be less readily accessible. Do you rely heavily on frequent support or input from others? Will you be a "fish out of water" working at home away from coworkers? Consider the following factors and rate them on a scale from high to low.

		Circle One	
1. Ability to work productively without needing supervision or frequent feedback	H	M	L
2. Initiative/Requests input when needed	H	M	L
3. Reliability and discipline regarding work commitments	H	M	L
4. Able to thrive in a work environment isolated from coworkers	H	M	L
5. Self-motivation/Self-discipline/Ability to avoid procrastination	H	M	L
6. Flexibility/Ability to work confidently in unfamiliar or constantly changing situations	H	M	L
7. Independence/Ability to self manage	H	M	L

Assessing Your Virtual Work Abilities

DIRECTIONS:

1. Use the information from the Telecommuting Personal Screener completed in the previous activity and the information you have read in the textbook chapter to help you evaluate your current abilities to work as a teleworker or virtual assistant.

   - Find at least one area of strength from each section of the screener (prerequisites, skills, and work style). List the areas of strength and describe why they are your strengths.

   - Find one or more areas from each section of the screener for which you gave yourself a low rating. List the areas of weakness and describe the steps you could take that would turn them into strengths.

2. Write a short reflection paper that includes the information you identified in the bullets above. Use an appropriate title and format the paper as an unbound report.

Assessment of Chapter Goals

DIRECTIONS: Review the Chapter 3 goals listed here. Did you successfully complete these goals? Evaluate yourself by completing the form below. If you did not satisfy the goal, state your reason(s) for not doing so.

1. Define *telework* and describe its benefits to teleworkers and organizations.

   Yes_____   No_____

2. Define *virtual assistant* and describe benefits and concerns for virtual assistant clients.

   Yes_____   No_____

3. Identify virtual workplace considerations including personal characteristics, virtual workforce skills, and challenges.

   Yes_____   No_____

4. Describe an effective work environment for virtual workers.

   Yes_____   No_____

Chapter 4   Your Professional Image

English and Word Usage Drill

DIRECTIONS: Review the Capitalization section of the Reference Guide of your textbook. Then correct the sentences below in the space provided. Some sentences may be correct as written. Cite the rule that applies.

1. The college of business is the largest one in the school.

   Rule

2. The holy trinity methodist church holds a special service each Sunday for the children.

   Rule

3. She purchased a Maytag washer and dryer.

   Rule

4. The session will take place in Mid-August.

   Rule

5. The Winter season is beautiful in Canada.

   Rule

6. Last week aunt Mary called to tell me that my cousin had a baby.

   Rule

7. Annette Yamamoto, vice president of Black, Inc., will be the keynote speaker at the graduation ceremony.

   Rule

8. My family visits new york city every thanksgiving and stays at the crown plaza hotel.

   Rule

9. The boston tea party was a protest by American colonists against Great Britain.

   Rule

10. We flew to Florida on Northwest Airlines Flight 1343.

   Rule

Case Study: Creating a Positive Professional Image

DIRECTIONS: Read the case below and respond to the questions. Discuss the case with three of your classmates. As a group write a summary of your responses and submit them to your instructor.

CASE:

Jose Garcia was hired six months ago in an entry-level sales position for United Pharmaceuticals. Although Jose is interested in sales, he eventually wants to move into a management position. For the most part, Jose thinks he is getting along well with his sales team and his supervisor.

Jose shares an office with Alex Franklin, one of his team members. Although Alex has made all of his monthly sales quotas, Jose notices that he arrives exactly at 8 a.m. and leaves immediately at 5 p.m. when the workday is over. He takes a coffee break at 10:15 a.m. and leaves for lunch exactly at noon regardless of his workload. Last week when the phone rang at 11:50 a.m. Alex did not answer because he had plans for lunch. When Alex was scheduled to attend a meeting on a Saturday morning, he called in "sick" the following Monday.

Jose has also noticed that in the last few weeks Alex has starting complaining about everything. In the last few days, he has made several negative comments about the required job duties. Last week Jose overheard Alex on the phone talking negatively about his supervisor. Jose has also noticed that people have started to avoid him when he is with Alex. In fact, yesterday when they walked into the break room, everyone left. Next week Alex has an interview in the Marketing Department with Mr. Edwardo Sanchez, the vice president of marketing. Alex has told you he really wants this job and has asked for your help.

QUESTIONS:

1. What tips can you give Alex to make a good first impression?

2. What suggestions can you give to Alex that will help him present a more positive attitude?

3. What changes can Alex make to his work ethic that would help him present a more professional image?

Maintaining Your Professional Image

DIRECTIONS: Analyze the following situations. Describe how you would handle each situation and explain your reasoning. Key your answers and print them to submit to your instructor.

Situation 1

You are at a formal business luncheon with your supervisor. The waitress asks if you would like an alcoholic drink.

Situation 2

A visitor whose appointment you forgot to cancel arrives as scheduled. Your supervisor is working under pressure to complete an important contract.

Situation 3

You are invited to an outdoor picnic at your supervisor's house after work, and the invitation says business casual. You have an important meeting in the morning and need to wear a business suit to work; you will not have time to change before the party.

Situation 4

You have made a rather serious error on a client's order. The client is not pleased about your error and calls your supervisor to complain.

Situation 5

It is five minutes before you typically leave for lunch. Your supervisor asks you to make 50 copies of a 15-page report that he needs for a meeting immediately after lunch.

Situation 6

You are scheduled to meet with a new client at 10 a.m. tomorrow. The client's office is on the other side of town in an unfamiliar area.

Situation 7

You are on the elevator with several colleagues, and your cell phone rings.

Situation 8

A client is meeting with your supervisor, and it is time for you to leave.

Introducing Others

DIRECTIONS: Five situations where introductions need to be made are shown in this activity. Several of the individuals are employees of United Pharmaceuticals. Refer to the information in Chapter 1 of this workbook if you need to know their titles or roles within the company. Read each of the following situations and write the appropriate introduction in the space following the situation.

Situation 1

You are at a business dinner. You are introducing Kimberly Loukinen, a new student assistant, to your supervisor, Melody Hoover.

Introduction

Situation 2

Mr. Leroy Sanchez, the president of the local Kiwanis club, is visiting your organization. You are introducing him to Teresa Winwright of United Pharmaceuticals.

Introduction

Situation 3

You are at a company dinner. You are introducing the state governor, Jacob Westmier, to David Anderson of United Pharmaceuticals.

Introduction

Situation 4

You are shopping with your grandmother, Mrs. Bethany Littleton, and you run into your supervisor, Amando Hinojosa.

Introduction

Situation 5

A committee of administrative assistants is meeting in your office to discuss upcoming contract negotiations. The administrative assistants are Jack Swanson, Ruth Lamers, and Willard Seagrave. They are meeting with Derek Syrjala, a representative from the Human Resources Department, and David Anderson from United Pharmaceuticals.

Introduction

Assessment of Chapter Goals

DIRECTIONS: Review the Chapter 4 goals listed here. Did you successfully complete these goals? Evaluate yourself by completing the form below. If you did not satisfy the goal, state your reason(s) for not doing so.

1. Describe the personal characteristics and work characteristics that contribute to a positive professional image.

    Yes_____   No_____

2. Identify the components of a professional appearance.

    Yes_____   No_____

3. Understand the conventions of business etiquette.

    Yes_____   No_____

Chapter 5   Anger, Stress, and Time Management

English and Word Usage Drill

DIRECTIONS: Review the Misused and Easily Confused Words and Phrases section in the Reference Guide of your textbook. Then correct the sentences below in the space provided. Some sentences may be correct as written. Cite the rule that applies.

1. She wrote her term paper a while ago.

   Rule

2. All of us are attending the concert on Friday evening.

   Rule

3. John told me he feels very badly about the accident.

   Rule

4. The decision was made between the three of us.

   Rule

5. Lansing is the capital of Michigan.

   Rule

6. Maria appraised me of the situation.

    Rule

7. We will attend the biennial meeting, which occurs twice a year.

    Rule

8. Mr. Park paid Mary Ann a complement on her dress.

    Rule

9. Mohammed is the person whom will speak next.

    Rule

10. The man scored 98 per cent on the test.

    Rule

5-2 Complete Stress and Anger Audits (Goal 3)

DIRECTIONS: For the anger audit, describe the behaviors and incidents as indicated below. When you are angry, for example, your face gets red, you yell, you strike people, you throw objects, or you sulk. Key each heading shown below and your response under each heading. Save them for use in a later activity.

ANGER AUDIT

Behaviors I Demonstrate When I Am Angry

Incidents That Made Me Angry This Past Week

Incidents That Made Me Angry This Past Month

5-4 Prepare an Action Plan (Goal 6)

DIRECTIONS: In preparation for creating an action plan, complete a time log. Using the forms provided here, log the time you spend in various activities for the next five days. Record each day's activities on a different form. If you are employed, log the time you spend in activities at work. If you are not employed, log the way you spend your personal time.

TIME LOG

DAY 1

TIME	TYPE OF ACTIVITY	TIME USED	PRIORITY	COMMENTS ON ACTIVITY

DAY 2

TIME	TYPE OF ACTIVITY	TIME USED	PRIORITY	COMMENTS ON ACTIVITY

DAY 3

TIME	TYPE OF ACTIVITY	TIME USED	PRIORITY	COMMENTS ON ACTIVITY

DAY 4

TIME	TYPE OF ACTIVITY	TIME USED	PRIORITY	COMMENTS ON ACTIVITY

DAY 5

TIME	TYPE OF ACTIVITY	TIME USED	PRIORITY	COMMENTS ON ACTIVITY

TIME MANAGEMENT ANALYSIS

DIRECTIONS: Referring to your daily time logs, analyze the way you spent your time during the five days. Key answers to the following questions.

1. What patterns and habits are apparent from my time log?

2. What was the most productive period of the day?

3. What was the least productive period of the day?

4. Who or what accounted for interruptions?

5. How can the interruptions be controlled or minimized?

6. What were the biggest time wasters?

7. How can the time wasters be eliminated or minimized?

8. On what activities can I spend less time?

9. What activities need more of my time?

ACTION PLAN

DIRECTIONS: Review the stress audit and the anger audit you prepared in Application 5-2 and the time log and analysis you prepared. Create an action plan, stating how you will seek to manage your stress, anger, and time during this semester. Key the plan title and the questions as shown below. Key the heading, the questions, and your responses to the questions and give the names of the team members with whom you worked.

STRESS, ANGER, AND TIME MANAGEMENT ACTION PLAN

1. I will manage my stress by engaging in the following activities:

2. I will manage my anger by engaging in the following activities:

3. I will manage my time by engaging in the following activities:

Team Members:

Case Study: Time Management

DIRECTIONS: Read the case below. Analyze Yuan's work habits and their effect on his productivity. Respond to the three questions in the space provided. Share your responses in a small group discussion with your class members.

CASE:

Yuan Chang works as a systems analyst and reports to Dianne Bradwell. Yuan was given a major project two months ago; it is due next month. Recently Dianne's workload increased dramatically due to the installation of a new computer system. Dianne calls Yuan to troubleshoot problems with the system. Because these problems affect employees' work production, Yuan must handle them promptly.

Yuan was planning to take a two-week vacation. However, he is behind on the project and has only four weeks left to finish it. He feels burned out due to his heavy workload. He tries to work on the project every day, but Dianne's calls keep him busy. He has not mentioned to Dianne that he is behind on the project. For the last two weeks, Yuan has been bringing a sandwich from home so he can work through lunch. He also stays late, working until at least 6 p.m. each day.

QUESTIONS:

1. Describe what may result if Yuan continues to handle his situation as he currently is.

2. How can Yuan manage his time more effectively?

3. Does Yuan need to talk with his supervisor about the situation? If so, what should he say to her?

Assessment of Chapter Goals

DIRECTIONS: Review the Chapter 5 goals listed here. Did you successfully complete these goals? Evaluate yourself by completing the form below. If you did not satisfy the goal, state your reason(s) for not doing so.

1. Determine the effects of stress in the workplace.

   Yes_____   No_____

2. Identify factors that contribute to workplace stress.

   Yes_____   No_____

3. Determine the purpose of anger and its resolution.

   Yes_____   No_____

4. Determine how time may be wasted.

   Yes_____   No_____

5. Describe the relationship among stress, anger, and time.

   Yes_____   No_____

6. Apply appropriate techniques for managing stress, anger, and time.

   Yes_____   No_____

Chapter 6   Ethical Theories and Behaviors

English and Word Usage Drill

DIRECTIONS: Review the Misused and Easily Confused Words and Phrases section in the Reference Guide of your textbook. Then correct the sentences below in the space provided. Some sentences may be correct as written. Cite the rule that applies.

1. My favorite desert is pumpkin pie.

    Rule

2. My house is two miles further from the museum than yours is.

    Rule

3. You may leave when you finish your work.

    Rule

4. Every six months, we need to replenish our supply of stationary.

    Rule

5. Alejandro is the person to who you should speak.

    Rule

6. They will accept our proposal at the meeting tomorrow.

    Rule

7. The counsel members will meet today to discuss the proposal.

    Rule

8. He will leave for the festival at about noon.

    Rule

9. The Franklin family had it's reunion yesterday.

    Rule

10. Jennings was not able to give the presentation, which should have been delivered to the managers.

    Rule

Making Ethical Decisions

DIRECTIONS: Analyze the following situations. Key answers to the question(s) given below each situation and submit them to your instructor.

Situation 1

As an administrative professional, you make hotel reservations for your employer at least three times a month. You use the same chain of hotels. You recently received a certificate from the local hotel chain offering you and your spouse a weekend getaway special, including a suite and breakfast each morning at no cost to you. Your company has no policy for accepting gifts, and your employer has not mentioned to you how gift offers should be handled.

- Is it ethical to take advantage of this offer? Why or why not?
- Should you tell your employer about the offer? Why or why not?

Situation 2

Sally (a friend of yours) works in the Marketing Department of a large company. She has been told the company has a rule that employees cannot accept gifts from suppliers, vendors, or customers—not even inexpensive gifts. She has noticed that her employer and several other company executives are invited each year to a golf tournament hosted by one of the company's vendors. All expenses are paid, and the event includes a nice meal after the tournament and numerous prizes. Her employer always comes back raving about the event and showing off the prizes he has won. Sally believes the company has set a double standard—one for the executives and one for the other employees. Sally likes her job and thinks the company is a good place to work.

- Should Sally let her supervisor know she believes the company has set a double standard or should she keep quiet? Give reasons for your answer.
- If you think she should tell him, how should she approach the subject with him?

Situation 3

Jane, one of your coworkers at United Pharmaceuticals, recently came to you with this story and asked your advice on what she should do.

Jane's supervisor, Mr. Thomas, asked her to have lunch with him to review the details of a workshop she was responsible for organizing. He suggested they go to the hotel where the workshop was to be held so she could look at the meeting setup possibilities. The lunch was very businesslike. When they started to leave, Mr. Thomas commented that it was too early to return to work. He asked, "Why don't we take some time to look at one of the hotel rooms?" Mr. Thomas winked at her as he said it, leaving no doubt as to what he was suggesting. Jane told Mr. Thomas she needed to get back to work. Smiling he responded, "I'll give you a rain check." Although Jane has worked for Mr. Thomas for two years, this was the first time he has made any advances. Jane does not know what to do.

- What advice would you give to Jane regarding having a romantic relationship with her employer?
- If Jane decides that the relationship is not appropriate or not wanted, how should she handle the situation?

Case Study: Workplace Ethics

DIRECTIONS: Read the case below and respond to the questions. Discuss the case with three of your classmates. As a group, write responses to the questions and submit them to your instructor in a memo. Use the *Word* file *Memo Form* provided on the Student CD.

CASE:

Ethan Zuroski accepted a position with a manufacturing company as an inventory clerk; he has been working there for six months. The company manufactures various types of glues. Ethan's office is in the facility where the glues are produced. As an inventory clerk, he is responsible for keeping a computer record of supplies used in the production process. He is in the plant frequently.

Recently Ethan has not been feeling well. He coughs frequently and has severe headaches. Additionally, he is nauseous to the point of vomiting. After seeing a medical doctor, he learns he is allergic to the products used in the manufacture of the glues.

Several of Ethan's coworkers tell him that other people have had problems but that they are afraid to report their concerns. The general feeling in the company is that management does not care about the workers.

Ethan has not been formally evaluated on the job; however, his supervisor has often told Ethan what a good job he is doing. Even though Ethan has heard rumors about the uncaring attitude of management, he discounts them because his supervisor has been so nice. After seeing the physician, Ethan tells his supervisor what the doctor said. A week later Ethan's supervisor informs him that his work is unsatisfactory and fires him with no notice. Ethan is shocked. He wonders what he should do.

QUESTIONS:

1. Do research on the Internet to learn about employee rights and employer rights. Based on what you have learned, do you think it is legal for the company to dismiss Ethan because of his health problems?

2. What steps can Ethan take to regain his job or seek damages for unfair treatment?

Customer Refunds

You work as an accounts receivable associate for Able Company. The company is committed to ethical treatment of all customers. Recently, the company installed a new software package for tracking payments on customer accounts. The software automatically applies discounts if payment is received within the discount period. For example, if a customer pays within ten days, the customer receives a 2 percent discount from the amount owed. The software default setting for discounts is 1 percent. When the software was installed, the setting should have been changed to 2 percent. Because the setting was not changed, several customers did not receive the full discount amount to which they were entitled. You have been asked to write a letter to customers explaining the situation and apologizing for the error. A list of customers that are affected by the error appears on page 53.

DIRECTIONS:

1. Create a spreadsheet to list the customers and to calculate the refund amount each customer is owed. Include the following data in columns in the spreadsheet. Note that three columns should be used for the contact person.

    Contact Person
        (Title, First Name, Last Name)
    Company Name
    Address
    City
    State
    ZIP Code
    Invoice Amount
    1% Discount
    2% Discount
    Refund Amount

2. Record the customer data from page 53 in the spreadsheet. For each customer, enter a formula to calculate the 1% discount, the 2% discount, and the refund amount. The refund amount will be the difference between the 1% and 2% discounts. Format numbers in the 1% Discount, 2% Discount, and Refund Amount columns for currency with two decimal places.

3. Write the body of a form letter to be sent to the customers. In the first paragraph, thank the company for its business and assure the company that it is a valued customer. In the second paragraph, apologize for a recent mistake regarding the customer's account. Explain to customers that they did not receive the proper payment discount on their last payment due to a processing error. State the amount of the refund that the customer is due. Give customers the option of having the refund amount applied to their accounts or receiving a refund check. In the last paragraph, ask customers to let you know which option they prefer. Also ask customers to call you if they have any questions about the refund and include your phone number: 606-555-1023.

4. Use the mail merge feature of your word processing software to create personalized letters for the customers.
   - Use the form letter for the body of the letter.
   - Use the current date.
   - Use the spreadsheet as the data source for the mail merge.
   - In the letter address, insert field codes for the contact person (title, first name, and last name), company name, address, city, state, and ZIP Code.
   - For the salutation, enter "Dear" and a field code for the contact person's title and last name.
   - Enter a field code for the refund amount in paragraph 2.
   - Format the letter in block style and use open punctuation. Refer to the Reference Guide in your textbook for example letter styles. Assume the letter will be printed on company letterhead stationery.
   - Complete the merge process and review the letters. Print the letters.

Name _____

Title	Contact Person		Company	Address	City	State	ZIP Code	Invoice Amount
	First Name	Last Name						
Mr.	Kyle	Anders	Anders and Son	Rt. 1 Box 210	Brodhead	KY	40409-5665	$525.50
Mr.	Logan	Carter	Redmond Associates	56 Walnut Street	Berea	KY	40403-5610	$348.00
Mr.	Tye	Chen	Creative Visions	528 Crawford Lane	Mt. Vernon	KY	40456-5281	$1,025.00
Ms.	Ollie	Depew	Brodhead Contractors	404 Moren Road	Brodhead	KY	40409-0404	$724.30
Mr.	Keith	Edwards	Edwards Landscaping	456 Dogwood Lane	Mt. Vernon	KY	40456-4561	$422.23
Mr.	Jesse	Garner	Ridge Contractors	89 Third Street	Brodhead	KY	40409-1189	$656.02
Mr.	Charles	Helton	A-1 Cleaning Service	781 Williams Street	Conway	KY	40456-2781	$550.25
Mr.	William	Jackson	Renfro Valley Antiques	952 Hall Drive	Mt. Vernon	KY	40456-9555	$689.42
Ms.	Maria	Juarez	Steak House	136 Abbey Lane	Mt. Vernon	KY	40456-1136	$445.69
Mr.	Jim	Kirk	Jim's Auto Repair	304 Starlight Way	Mt. Vernon	KY	40456-1304	$712.30
Ms.	Dana	Lee	Lee's Bakery	Rt. 3 Box 247	Mt. Vernon	KY	40456-0247	$521.00
Mr.	Antonio	Martinez	Old Town Weavers	34 Pearl Street	Berea	KY	40403-3334	$389.25
Mr.	Jack	Matthews	Jack's Pools	P.O. Box 495	Mt. Vernon	KY	40456-0495	$125.50
Ms.	Gail	McConnell	River Excursions	308 River Road	Conway	KY	40456-0308	$165.34
Mr.	Danny	O'Malley	Village Arts	442 Wood Street	Mt. Vernon	KY	40456-1442	$890.12
Mr.	Joe	Pace	Pace Auto	872 Greenway Drive	Mt. Vernon	KY	40456-8721	$124.89
Ms.	Keto	Park	Park Heating Systems	445 Woodland Place	Mt. Vernon	KY	40456-0445	$542.65
Ms.	Carolyn	Phelps	Brodhead Quick Stop	32 Knox Avenue	Brodhead	KY	40409-0032	$345.50
Mr.	Randall	Raines	Cumberland Gift Shop	88 Ray Hill Road	Renfro Valley	KY	40473-1188	$189.56
Mr.	Al	Santos	Taco Stop	561 Hale Street	Mt. Vernon	KY	40456-5612	$456.78
Mr.	Blaine	Thomson	Wood Crafts	92 Elm Street	Berea	KY	40403-9231	$225.40
Ms.	Barbara	Willis	Kentucky Baskets and Quilts	382 South Street	Berea	KY	40403-1736	$3,505.75
Ms.	Alice	Yung	Rockcastle Crafts	156 West Street	Mt. Vernon	KY	40456-0156	$2,550.50

Assessment of Chapter Goals

DIRECTIONS: Review the Chapter 6 goals listed here. Did you successfully complete these goals? Evaluate yourself by completing the form below. If you did not satisfy the goal, state your reason(s) for not doing so.

1. Explain the importance of ethical behavior in the workplace.

    Yes_____   No_____

2. Identify characteristics of an ethical organization.

    Yes_____   No_____

3. Determine how to achieve ethical change.

    Yes_____   No_____

4. Determine implications of discrimination in an organization.

    Yes_____   No_____

5. Identify characteristics of an ethical employee.

    Yes_____   No_____

6. Determine your commitment to ethical behavior.

    Yes_____   No_____

Chapter 7   Written Communications

English and Word Usage Drill

DIRECTIONS: Review the Proofreader's Marks section of the Reference Guide of your textbook. Then key or write the sentences below, making the corrections indicated.

1. The Meeting is scheduled to begin at Noon on Friday.

2. The turnaround time for the reprographic department has been decreased significantly.

3. Yesterday the beautiful sun was shining.

4. The project was continuing to progress despite the delay in funding.

5. Installation of the local area network (lan) is scheduled for next month.

6. Marci is the most efficient worker on our team.

7. At the ball game, 8 players hit home runs.   sp

8. Dr Jones and Dr Martinez arrived on time

9. A comma is used to separate parenthetical expressions from the rest of a sentence.

10. Our winter break begins on december 20.

7-3 Write Business Letters

DIRECTIONS: Compose letters for the following situations, following the instructions in your textbook.

Situation A

Write a letter to Mr. Roger Edwards, 984 Fourth Street, Fort Worth, TX 76101-2403, inviting him to speak to a group of administrative professionals from United Pharmaceuticals on November 8 at 7:30 p.m. about management theory and practices. You are to sign the letter. Your title is Administrative Assistant. Date the letter one month before the meeting.

Situation B

Write a letter to Mr. David VanderFleet, 2005 Fifth Street, Fort Worth, TX 76101-2803, asking him to be on a panel with Teresa Winwright to discuss the future directions of cancer research. The presentation is to be given to the South Lake Chamber of Commerce on (put in date one month from the current date); the session will begin with lunch and conclude at approximately 2 p.m. Mr. VanderFleet is to explain the direction that United Pharmaceuticals is taking on cancer research. His presentation should be no more than 30 minutes, with a 10-minute question-and-answer session. Teresa Winwright will sign the letter. Date the letter with the current date.

Situation C

Assume David VanderFleet has said "yes" to the request in Situation B. Write a second letter to him acknowledging his positive response. Tell him that Teresa Winwright will meet him at the South Lake Chamber, 2300 Winsor Road, South Lake at 11:50 a.m. on the meeting date. Also tell him that Teresa will call him next Thursday at 9 a.m. to discuss the presentation. Ask him to suggest another time if he is not available at this particular time. Teresa Winwright will sign the letter. Date the letter one week from the current date.

Case Study: Improve Written Communications

DIRECTIONS: Read the case below and answer the questions. Revise the letter as directed in the last question.

CASE:

You have a friend who works for the local county tax assessment office as an administrative assistant to the director. The office employs, in addition to the director, two additional administrative assistants and five assessors. Your friend handles most of the correspondence to county residents concerning increased property assessments. She follows a format given to her by the previous person in her position.

Most of the correspondence can follow a standard format by simply changing names, addresses, and assessed property values. Some letters, however, are written to clarify property transactions and inform residents of increased valuations. The director receives numerous complaints from citizens about the letters sent from the assessment office. The citizens complain that the letters are negative in tone, contain incorrect information, and include grammatical errors. Due to the large volume of letters, the director cannot read every word of every letter before he signs them.

Your friend uses her spelling and grammar tools, but she does not check the accuracy of the increased valuations. She keys what the director gives her. A review of the last five letters shows that she missed errors in word usage, misspelled the taxpayer's name, and incorrectly keyed the increased property valuation. A first draft of a letter written by your friend is shown on the following page. Your friend asks you to read and evaluate the letter.

QUESTIONS:

1. After reading this letter and the situation, what suggestions would you make to your friend?

2. Should your friend make any suggestions to the director? If so, what?

3. How can you improve this written communication? Key the letter, revising it to use an indirect approach and a positive tone.

FIRST DRAFT

December 15, 200-

Mr. Thomas A. Alexander
3459 Pine Lake Drive
Euless, TX 76033-3459

Dear Mr. Alexender:

Unfortunately, the accessed value of your home at 3495 Pine Lake Drive has increased.
There has been an increase in the assessed value of all property in your area of at least 10
percent. However, because your home is the newest one in the area, your accessed value
has increased 15 percent. The tax statement that you receive in January will reflect this
increase.

If you has any questions, you may call my office.

Sincerely

Robert Edwards
Director

Letter with Indirect Approach

DIRECTIONS:

1. Write a letter declining an invitation that has been extended to you to speak to the local chapter of IAAP next month. Because this letter will contain news with which the reader may be disappointed, use the indirect writing approach.

   - Use the United Pharmaceuticals letterhead that you created earlier.
   - Use modified block letter format and open punctuation.
   - Use the current date for the letter.
   - Address the letter to:
     Ms. Anna Garcia
     IAAP Program Chairperson
     123 Maple Street
     (Use your city, state, and ZIP Code)

   - Acknowledge Ms. Garcia's request for you to speak. (Mention a particular month and day for the meeting that is at least one month from today.) Thank her for the invitation.
   - State that you will not be able to speak when requested due to the press of work. Include some details regarding your current commitments. Offer to speak the following month.
   - Include other details or comments that you think are appropriate.
   - Use your name and the title *Administrative Assistant* in the signature block.

2. Ask a classmate to critique and proofread your letter. Make corrections as needed before printing a final copy.

Assessment of Learning Goals

DIRECTIONS: Review the Chapter 7 goals listed here. Did you successfully complete these goals? Evaluate yourself by completing the form below. If you did not satisfy the goal, state your reason(s) for not doing so.

1. Compose written communications.

   Yes_____   No_____

2. Apply characteristics of effective correspondence.

   Yes_____   No_____

3. Apply appropriate planning and writing guidelines.

   Yes_____   No_____

4. Engage in collaborative writing and research.

   Yes_____   No_____

Chapter 8   Verbal Communication and Presentations

English and Word Usage Drill

DIRECTIONS: Review the usage rules in the Numbers section of the Reference Guide of your textbook. Then correct the sentences below. Some sentences may be correct as written. Cite the rule that applies.

1. Ray bought 3 reference books, 2 writing books, and 1 math book.

    Rule

2. I ordered 10 reams of paper, 11 boxes of envelopes, and eighteen pens.

    Rule

3. A few 100 voters turned out for the candidate's speech.

    Rule

4. The student is nine years old.

    Rule

5. The meeting will be on June 5th.

    Rule

6. The check was written for $1,045.63.

   Rule

7. The recipe called for one fourth cup of sugar.

   Rule

8. 300 fans attended the baseball game.

   Rule

9. The population of the region has reached 3,000,000,000.

   Rule

10. The average score on the test was eighty-seven %.

    Rule

Case Study: Communication in the Workplace

DIRECTIONS: In your part-time position with United Pharmaceuticals, you recently had a problem with Melody Hoover. Read the case below and consider the questions. Write a summary of your responses in a memo to your instructor. Use the Word file *Memo Form* found on the Student CD to prepare the memo.

CASE:

You were 25 minutes late for work on Tuesday, and you did not call in to report that you would be late. Why? You understood from Melody that you did not need to call if you were going to be less than 30 minutes late. When you arrived at the office, you quickly explained that you were delayed in one of your classes. Melody responded with an "okay," but she had a frown on her face when she said it. She then gave you an assignment and told you she needed it back in 30 minutes.

You took the assignment and began reviewing it. However, you soon discovered that you did not have all the information you needed to complete the assignment. You thought it best not to bother Melody again when she seemed stressed. Instead, you went to the file and pulled information that seemed to pertain to the assignment. You completed the task within 30 minutes and placed it on Melody's desk. (She was not at her desk when you did so.)

When Melody returned, she looked at your work and said, "I need to talk with you." At this point, her facial expression and tone of voice indicated she was quite angry. She said, "This work is not satisfactory. My supervisor is waiting for this work. You have placed me in a most awkward position. The next time you do not understand an assignment, tell me." You were so upset that you said nothing. Melody took the work and started redoing it. She said very little to you the remainder of the day.

QUESTIONS:

1. What is the first communication problem in the situation? What should you do regarding this problem?

2. What should you have done differently regarding the work assignment?

3. What should you have done differently or what should you do now in response to Melody's comments about the work being unsatisfactory?

4. What can you do in general to improve your communication with Melody?

Resolving Conflict

DIRECTIONS: Think of a situation that involved a conflict. The situation could be one in which you were involved personally or one you read about or viewed on television. Key answers to the following questions regarding the conflict situation.

1. Who were the people involved in the conflict?

2. Describe the conflict situation. What was the cause or underlying issues of the conflict?

3. Did you or a participant in the conflict listen and talk with others to try to understand the conflict? If yes, describe what took place.

4. Did the people involved seem able to separate the people from the issues in the conflict? Discuss the situation.

5. Was the conflict resolved? If yes, describe how the conflict was resolved. If no, tell why you think no resolution was reached.

6. What could you or another person who was involved have done differently to improve communication and help resolve the conflict?

Assessment of Learning Goals

DIRECTIONS: Review the Chapter 8 goals listed here. Did you successfully complete these goals? Evaluate yourself by completing the form below. If you did not satisfy the goal, state your reason(s) for not doing so.

1. Identify elements of effective verbal communication.

    Yes_____   No_____

2. Demonstrate effective verbal and nonverbal communication.

    Yes_____   No_____

3. Explain how effective communication can help resolve conflicts.

    Yes_____   No_____

4. Prepare and deliver a verbal presentation using visuals.

    Yes_____   No_____

Chapter 9   Customer Service

English and Word Usage Drill

DIRECTIONS: Review the usage rules in the Parallelism section of the Reference Guide of your textbook. Then correct the sentences below. Some sentences may be correct as written.

1. The children's program included reading, acting, and songs.

2. The job involves talking with customers, phone calls, and writing letters.

3. Each day of the triathlon consisted of either jogging and swimming or on the bike and jogging.

4. The game was stimulating and a challenge.

5. The printer is light, efficient, and it is relatively inexpensive.

6. The employees have already started using new methods and to increase productivity.

7. If you are uncertain about how to handle mail, you should research the process, consult with your employer, or you should ask a colleague.

8. The seminar will address:
   • How to use new equipment.
   • Coping with stress.
   • What the standards for productivity should be.

9. The team talked with employees, read reports, and conducted research.

10. When reading for main ideas, skim titles and headings; when you want to remember details, reading all text carefully is required.

Case Study: Customer Service

DIRECTIONS: Read the case below and answer the questions that follow the case.

CASE:

Melissa decided to buy a sewing machine to take to quilting classes. The machine she already had was both heavy and expensive. She did not want to risk damaging it during travel. She decided that the new machine should weigh less than 10 pounds and have a sturdy carrying case to keep it safe during travel. The machine should have a bright light to eliminate the need for taking a lamp to classes. Before ordering a new sewing machine online, Melissa read the product descriptions for several sewing machines carefully. She also compared prices. She selected a machine that, according to the product description, would fill her needs. The Web page described the machine as having a hard carrying case, a super bright light, and several accessories made especially for quilting. The machine was also within the weight requirements.

When the sewing machine arrived, Melissa thought at first that she must have been sent the wrong item. The machine had a hard cover that sat loosely over it—not a case in which the machine would fit securely for travel. She also found that the light (in her opinion) was not super bright but very dim. The promised quilting accessories were not included.

Melissa called the customer support line for the company from which she ordered the machine. She explained that the item was not as she expected from reading the production description on the Website (case and light) and that the quilting accessories were not included. She explained to the customer service representative (CSR) that she chose this machine, in large part, because of the carrying case that was supposed to be included. She requested that she be allowed to return the item. The CSR agreed that Melissa could return the machine, but she said that Melissa would be charged a 15 percent restocking fee because the box had been opened. The conversation continued from there:

Melissa (surprised)	Well, of course I opened the box the machine arrived in. How else could I look at the item?
CSR:	Our Website states that return of any opened item will be subject to a restocking fee.
Melissa:	My understanding from reading your Web page was that this would apply only to items such as software or other packaged items. However, even if it is your normal policy for all items, I don't think I should be charged a fee for returning an item that is not as described on the Website.
CSR (in a matter-of-fact tone)	That is the description that came from the sewing machine manufacturer. You must just not understand what a case is or be able to judge whether a light is bright or not. You must pay the restocking fee if you wish to return the item.
Melissa:	Very well. I will return the item and would like a refund for the amount less the restocking fee issued to my credit card.
CSR:	I can give you a store credit for this item but not a refund to your credit card.

Melissa (very frustrated):	But, Miss, your Website says that items can be returned for store credit OR a refund.
CSR:	Perhaps that is true; however, for this item you can only get store credit.
Melissa (angry):	Okay. Send me the store credit. I will use it to buy some simple items such as needles or thread that cannot easily be misrepresented. After that I will never buy from your site again.
CSR:	I'm sorry you feel that way. I am only following our store policies.
Melissa (calmer now):	I realize that you have to follow your store policies. I realize that any company can have a mistake in a product description. However, your company should not expect customers to pay for its mistakes. I can order a sewing machine and supplies from at least three other companies that offer a 100 percent satisfaction guarantee. If I am not pleased for any reason, I can return the items for a full refund to my credit card. Those companies will have my business in the future.

QUESTIONS:

1. What were the communication problems in this situation? What should the company do regarding these problems to improve customer service?

2. What might the CSR have done differently regarding this situation?

3. Do you think the company in this situation has a true commitment to customer service? Why or why not?

4. What might Melissa have done differently in this situation?

Web Customer Service

DIRECTIONS:

1. Access the Internet and look at Websites for several retail companies. Read the return policy for each company and the satisfaction guarantee if one is given. Find how to contact customer service for the company.

2. Find at least two companies that you think demonstrate a commitment to customer service by their return and refund policies, their satisfaction guarantees, and the ease with which the company can be contacted. For each company, key a summary of the information you find (including the Website name and address) or print the Web page that contains the relevant information.

3. Find at least two companies that you think demonstrate a lack of commitment to customer service. Look at their return and refund policies, their satisfaction guarantees, and the methods and times available for contacting the company. For each company, key a summary of the information you find (including the Website name and address) or print the Web page that contains the relevant information.

Customer Service Letters

DIRECTIONS: You work for a small company called Cumberland Crafts. The store sells supplies for many types of hobbies and crafts such as painting, woodworking, and sewing. Customers can join a frequent buyer club. Members of the club receive a newsletter and special offers. You have been asked to send a letter to customers in the club who purchased $250 or more in merchandise during the past year.

1. Write the body of a form letter to be sent to the customers.
    *   Assume the letter will be printed on company letterhead stationery. Format the letter in block style and use open punctuation. Refer to the Reference Guide in your textbook for example letter styles.
    *   Use January 15 of the current year as the date. The letter address will come from a data source file. Enter *Dear* for the salutation. The name will come from a data source file.
    *   In the first paragraph, thank customers for being part of the Cumberland Crafts Club. Tell them that because they purchased $250 or more in merchandise last year, the company is pleased to offer them a special discount on their next order.
    *   In the second paragraph, explain the discount offer. The offer provides a 20 percent discount on their order/purchase of up to $500. The discount can be used on all merchandise at regular and sale prices. Customers should bring this letter if buying in person. If buying online, customers should enter the coupon code CCC250 in the checkout screen. State that the discount offer is not transferrable and can be used only once.
    *   In the third paragraph, tell customers that you hope they will take advantage of this offer to stock up on their favorite items and supplies. State that the offer is good through March 31 of the current year.
    *   Include an appropriate closing. Use your name and the title *Customer Care Associate* in the signature block.

2. Use a database or spreadsheet program to create a data source file for the customers' information. Record the customer data from the following page in the database table or spreadsheet. The state for all addresses is KY.

3. Use the mail merge feature of your word processing software to create personalized letters for the customers.
    *   Use the form letter you wrote earlier for the body of the letter.
    *   Use the database or spreadsheet you created earlier as the data source for the mail merge.
    *   In the letter address, insert field codes for the title, first name, last name, address, city, state, and ZIP Code.
    *   For the salutation, after "Dear" enter a field code for the person's title and last name.
    *   Complete the merge process and review the letters. Print the letters.

Title	First Name	Last Name	Address	City	ZIP Code
Mr.	Kyle	Anders	Rt. 1 Box 210	Brodhead	40409-5665
Mr.	Logan	Carter	56 Walnut Street	Berea	40403-5610
Ms.	Ollie	Depew	404 Moren Road	Brodhead	40409-0404
Mr.	Keith	Edwards	456 Dogwood Lane	Mt. Vernon	40456-4561
Ms.	Jessica	Garner	89 Third Street	Brodhead	40409-1189
Mr.	Charles	Helton	781 Williams Street	Conway	40456-2781
Ms.	Wilma	Jackson	952 Hall Drive	Mt. Vernon	40456-9555
Ms.	Maria	Juarez	136 Abbey Lane	Mt. Vernon	40456-1136
Mr.	Jim	Kirk	304 Starlight Way	Mt. Vernon	40456-1304
Ms.	Dana	Lee	Rt. 3 Box 247	Mt. Vernon	40456-0247
Mr.	Antonio	Martinez	34 Pearl Street	Berea	40403-3334
Mr.	Jack	Matthews	P.O. Box 495	Mt. Vernon	40456-0495
Ms.	Gail	McConnell	308 River Road	Conway	40456-0308
Mr.	Danny	O'Malley	442 Wood Street	Mt. Vernon	40456-1442
Mr.	Joe	Pace	872 Greenway Drive	Mt. Vernon	40456-8721
Ms.	Keto	Park	445 Woodland Place	Mt. Vernon	40456-0445
Ms.	Carolyn	Phelps	32 Knox Avenue	Brodhead	40409-0032
Mr.	Randall	Raines	88 Ray Hill Road	Renfro Valley	40473-1188
Ms.	Alicia	Santos	561 Hale Street	Mt. Vernon	40456-5612
Mr.	Blaine	Thomson	92 Elm Street	Berea	40403-9231
Ms.	Barbara	Willis	382 South Street	Berea	40403-1736
Ms.	Susie	Yung	156 West Street	Mt. Vernon	40456-0156

Assessment of Learning Goals

DIRECTIONS: Review the Chapter 9 goals listed here. Did you successfully complete these goals? Evaluate yourself by completing the form below. If you did not satisfy the goal, state your reason(s) for not doing so.

1. Describe the importance of effective customer service to an organization.

    Yes_____   No_____

2. Identify characteristics of companies that value customer service.

    Yes_____   No_____

3. Develop effective customer service skills.

    Yes_____   No_____

Chapter 10   Technology Update

English and Word Usage Drill

DIRECTIONS: Review the Plurals and Possessives section in the Reference Guide of your textbook. Then correct the sentences below in the space provided. Some sentences may be correct as written. Cite the rule that applies.

1. Drs. Pagel and Johnson research suggests a new direction for diabetes treatment.

    Rule

2. She will complete yours tomorrow.

    Rule

3. The runner-ups in the contest went out to dinner.

    Rule

4. Mr. and Mrs. Montoyas party was a huge success.

    Rule

5. The children are proficient in the three R's.

    Rule

6. The jury listened to the witnesses' contradictions.

   Rule

7. The children were laughing because Raymonds snoring was so loud.

   Rule

8. Her father-in-laws car was stolen.

   Rule

9. Dotting the *is* is essential.

   Rule

10. The dog was so sick that we needed to take her to the vet's.

    Rule

Case Study: Computer Passwords and Security

DIRECTIONS: Read the case below and respond to the questions. Discuss the case with three of your classmates. As a group, write responses to the questions and submit them to your instructor in a memo. Use the *Memo Form* provided on the Student CD.

CASE:

A computer network connects all the departments at United Pharmaceuticals. The Computer Department staff maintains and services software that resides on the system, troubleshoots hardware and technical problems, and monitors the agency's communications. Every employee with a computer logs in to the system with a network name assigned by the Computer Department and a secret password, which is chosen by the employee. Employees are required to change their passwords on the first working day of each month.

Rachelle Diego, an administrative assistant in the Grand Rapids division, spends a great deal of time on the computer and has access to much confidential human resources information. All of her coworkers know Rachelle has two children, Carlos and Rocio. In the lunchroom last week, Rachelle was overheard telling a new employee about the system she uses to set her password. In fact, Rachelle stated that she often uses one of her children's names as her password so the password is always easy to remember.

Jasper Yee, one of Rachelle's coworkers, has repeatedly asked Rachelle to find out the new department head's salary. Although Rachelle has refused, over the last week she learned that Jasper found the information he was seeking. Angry about the new department head's salary, Jasper has been complaining to anyone in the department who will listen. Rachelle's coworkers believe she has given Jasper the information he was seeking and are avoiding her in the lunchroom. Rachelle confronts Jasper and accuses him of using her password. Jasper adamantly denies using Rachelle's information to access the system.

QUESTIONS:

1. Did Rachelle handle the situation appropriately? If not, what could she have done differently?

2. Can Rachelle learn whether Jasper accessed the system using her password? Should she file a complaint if she learns someone has been using her password?

3. What other problems could this situation have created?

4. What company policies should be put in place as a result of this situation?

Memo Report on Email Use

The Marketing Department at United Pharmaceuticals is concerned with the amount of time employees spend working with email. Although they have not kept detailed data in the past, they think individuals spend more time on email if they check their messages randomly throughout the day than they would if they accessed their email only four times a day. For the past two weeks, a small group of employees have been asked to keep track of the number of minutes spent working with email. You will compare the two methods and recommend one for use by employees.

1. During the first week, employees checked their email as often as they wanted. Enter the following data into a spreadsheet.

MINUTES SPENT HANDLING EMAIL Week 1					
Name	Monday	Tuesday	Wednesday	Thursday	Friday
Ricardo Alvarez	125	105	100	115	103
Ellen Chang	130	99	101	87	115
Francise Haslitt	122	110	115	110	113
Warren Leroy	99	104	87	95	102
Mica Lombardini	118	128	131	125	117
Vincent Newman	121	98	99	102	105
Marshall Parks	88	97	89	78	87

2. Find the total number of minutes each employee spent on email during the week. Find the total hours all employees spent using the email program for week 1. Find the percent of time at work that was spent working with email for all employees. (Assume they all worked 40 hours that week.) Round the percents to two decimal places.

3. During the second week, employees were encouraged to check their email only four times a day at 8 a.m., 10 a.m., 2 p.m., and 4 p.m. The employees reported spending the following number of minutes working with email. Add this information to the spreadsheet.

MINUTES SPENT HANDLING EMAIL Week 2					
Name	Monday	Tuesday	Wednesday	Thursday	Friday
Ricardo Alvarez	92	86	74	91	97
Ellen Chang	130	117	108	114	133
Francise Haslitt	100	98	78	98	100
Warren Leroy	80	75	75	80	90
Mica Lombardini	130	115	90	95	92
Vincent Newman	100	80	78	83	100
Marshall Parks	105	112	98	102	114

4. Calculate the total minutes each employee spent on email for the week. Find the total hours all employees spent using the email program for week 2. Find the percent of time at work that was spent working with email for all employees. (Assume they all worked 40 hours that week.) Round the percents to two decimal places.

5. Create a column chart that compares the total number of hours the employees spent on email during week 1 to the total number of hours the employees spent on email during week 2. Title the chart *EMAIL TIME COMPARISON*. Display data labels for the columns.

6. Create a memo to Teresa Winwright, Vice President of Marketing at United Pharmaceuticals, from you, using the *Memo Form* file found on the Student CD. Use today's date and an appropriate subject line. Answer the following questions in the memo. Complete additional calculations as needed.
   - How did the change in email access affect the amount of time individuals spent checking their email?
   - What was the average amount of weekly work time employees spent checking email during week 1? What was the average amount of weekly work time employees spent checking email during week 2?
   - Which system appears to be the most efficient? Why?
   - Are there potential problems associated with the system used in week 2? If yes, describe them.
   - Are there other variables that may account for the differences between week 1 and week 2? If yes, describe them.

   Include the chart you created in the body of the memo to support your information. Make a recommendation as to whether the company should move toward this type of system.

Working with Utility Programs

Understanding the function of utility programs that are part of your computer's operating system and other utility programs will help you use your computer efficiently and keep it in good working order. You will explore and practice using a utility program in this activity.

DIRECTIONS:

1. Choose a utility program from the types listed below (or one that has been approved by your instructor).
   - File management programs
   - Search tools
   - Diagnostic and disk management programs
   - Disk defragmenter
   - Uninstall utilities
   - File compression programs
   - Virus scanners
   - Encryption utilities

2. Create a handout that includes the following information.
   - The program name and publisher
   - A description of the purpose of the program
   - Step-by-step instructions on how to use some feature or process of the program

3. When you have created the handout, ask one of your classmates to check your instructions for clarity and accuracy. Your instructor may also ask you to demonstrate your instructions to the class.

Assessment of Chapter Goals

DIRECTIONS: Review the Chapter 10 goals listed here. Did you successfully complete these goals? Evaluate yourself by completing the form below. If you did not satisfy the goal, state your reason(s) for not doing so.

1. Describe types of computers, input devices, storage devices, and networks commonly found in businesses.

   Yes_____   No_____

2. Describe the function of applications software and systems software.

   Yes_____   No_____

3. Understand threats and solutions related to computer security and privacy.

   Yes_____   No_____

Chapter 11   Workplace Mail and Copying

English and Word Usage Drill

DIRECTIONS: Review the punctuation rules for using periods and commas in the Reference Guide of your textbook. Then correct the sentences below. Some sentences may be correct as written. Cite the rule that applies.

1. Ms Lucy Whitman vice president for public relations will handle your request.

    Rule

2. Our new software program will let you send email transfer files manage appointments and make telephone calls.

    Rule

3. The advisory board meeting will begin at 9 am and conclude at 3 pm.

    Rule

4. The next time the national conference will be in Phoenix Arizona is October 25 2010 at the Dryden Hotel.

    Rule

5. We would like to make a decision by the end of the week but we need further information.

    Rule

6. The festival scheduled for May, 2009, will be held in the park.

   Rule

7. She however would not agree to the change.

   Rule

8. She said "I will be happy to complete the project."

   Rule

9. For example the copier will make color copies.

   Rule

10. Thank you Ms. Perez for accepting our offer.

    Rule

Case Study: Handling Confidential Mail

DIRECTIONS: Read the case below and respond to the questions.

CASE:

The mail is delivered to your office twice a day at 10 a.m. and 2 p.m. Kurt, another administrative assistant, usually handles all incoming mail. However, he will not be available today. He has asked that you handle Mrs. Patel's mail. Mrs. Patel is out of the office, but she will return early this evening to review the mail.

Several items are in the afternoon mail. You carefully open all the mail and check for enclosures. You complete the preliminary mail sort, open the items, and date and time-stamp them. Now you begin to read and annotate the mail. The first letter you are annotating requests that Mrs. Patel attend a meeting the following Monday. You underline the date in the letter and mark it on the calendar. As you continue to read the letter, you realize that the letter is about her child and that the meeting is scheduled with the school counselor and the principal. You check the envelope and notice it is marked *Personal and Confidential*. It is clear that the letter is not business related.

QUESTIONS:

1. What should you have done to avoid this problem?

2. How should you handle the situation? Explain what you should do to correct the problem.

Ethical Considerations Memo

You have been with your company for six months; you are an assistant to one of the vice presidents. Before joining the company, you worked as an administrative professional for five years. You like your supervisor. She has supported you and has told you that you are doing a good job. However, you have growing concerns about what is happening in the company and in your workplace. Here are some of your concerns:

- After only a few weeks on the job, you were asked by your employer to make three copies of a new software package for the other office professionals in your area. You made the copies.

- Your supervisor has repeatedly given you articles from magazines and books and asked you to make several copies. She has then told you to send the articles out to her colleagues across the nation. You have done so.

- Today the president of the company came into your office after a meeting with your supervisor. He handed you a book and asked that you copy and send 15 copies of Chapter 6 to a list of administrators. You made the copies and mailed them.

DIRECTIONS: Write a memo to Ms. Sanchez, your supervisor. Discuss your concerns about the ethics of making and distributing copies of software, articles, and books without permission from the copyright holders. Suggest how you think similar situations should be handled in the future to respect the copyrights of others and to be in compliance with copyright laws. Use the *Memo Form* provided on the Student CD to create the memo.

Research Fax Machines

DIRECTIONS:

1. Your department needs to replace its aging fax machine with a newer model. Use the Internet to find information about two fax machines that you think will meet the department's needs. The machine should use plain paper and be able to receive faxes at night when the workplace is closed. Any other features you think are necessary should also be included.

2. Write a memo to your supervisor, Mr. Chin. Describe two fax machines that you think would be appropriate. Include the cost of each machine, a general description, and any special features of each machine. Make a recommendation for the machine you think the department should purchase and state the reasons for your choice. Use the *Memo Form* provided on the Student CD to create the memo.

Assessment of Chapter Goals

DIRECTIONS: Review the Chapter 11 goals listed here. Did you successfully complete these goals? Evaluate yourself by completing the form below. If you did not satisfy the goal, state your reason(s) for not doing so.

1. Identify United States Postal Service mail classifications and services.

    Yes_____   No_____

2. Identify mail services available through private mail carriers.

    Yes_____   No_____

3. Process incoming and outgoing mail.

    Yes_____   No_____

4. Identify uses and features of copiers.

    Yes_____   No_____

5. Discuss the importance of ethical and legal considerations when copying and shredding materials.

    Yes_____   No_____

Chapter 12   Telecommunications–Technology and Etiquette

English and Word Usage Drill

DIRECTIONS: Review the Punctuation Rules for the semicolon and colon in the Reference Guide of your textbook. Then correct the sentences below. Some sentences may be correct as written. Cite the rule that applies.

1. I have a special fondness for the ocean it reminds me of the many happy summers we spent vacationing with my parents.

    Rule

2. At the job interview I learned that the company offers several important benefits for example, free dental insurance, family care leave, and a health club membership.

    Rule

3. The following software should be updated this year word processing, spreadsheet, and database.

    Rule

4. The luncheon is scheduled for 12 15 p.m. on Friday, June 1.

    Rule

5. Next year we will open satellite offices in Boston, Massachusetts Marquette, Michigan and Minneapolis, Minnesota.

Rule

6. We discussed a name for the clubhouse however, we could not come to an agreement.

Rule

7. Most of the students appreciated the conference day the teachers did not.

Rule

8. The following staff members have been with the company for more than 25 years Lucy Schwemin, Korey Lafayette, and Eunice Banks.

Rule

9. The job you have described sounds wonderful it is exactly the kind of job I had in mind.

Rule

10. Yesterday I placed an order for the following computer paper, black pens, and a toner cartridge.

Rule

Case Study: Voice Messaging

DIRECTIONS: Read the case below and answer the questions that follow the case.

CASE:

Celia Mesa works as an administrative professional for a small law firm, McKay, Carlson & Duffy. Celia started with the firm five years ago when there was only one attorney. Although the firm is still relatively small, there are three attorneys, and the number of clients has increased by 300 percent from five years ago.

One of Celia's responsibilities is to answer all incoming calls. There is one other administrative assistant in the office (added in the third year of operation), but the person has no phone responsibilities. In addition to answering the phone, Celia takes care of a myriad of other duties, including keying legal documents and filing correspondence. Celia finds it difficult to answer the calls in a timely manner. Several times this week the phone rang five or more times before she was able to get to it. There were several other instances where the caller hung up before Celia answered the phone. Celia also finds it difficult to keep up with her other duties. She has had to work extra hours every week for the last three months to complete keyboarding jobs and the filing is at least three months behind.

Mr. McKay was the founder of the firm, and he believes that providing a personal touch is important. He wants the employees to care about the clients. He rejected using a voice messaging system in the past because he considered it too impersonal. Celia is overloaded. She is going to have to ask for additional help—either a third person or a voice messaging system. She knows the voice messaging system would be less costly.

QUESTIONS:

1. What information regarding her workload does Celia need to make clear to Mr. McKay?

2. What type of cost information can Celia give to Mr. McKay to aid him in solving the problem?

Handling Calls Effectively

DIRECTIONS: Your supervisor, Melody Hoover, is out of the office and has put you in charge of the phones for the day. Analyze the following situations and determine an appropriate response. Key your responses and submit them to your instructor. (Note: You may find the information in Chapter 1 of this *Applications Workbook* labeled "YOUR ORGANIZATION" helpful when making your decisions.)

Situation 1

Ms. Winwright leaves the office at 11:30 a.m. for a luncheon with the Fort Worth mayor. She tells you she will return at approximately 2:30 p.m. The luncheon is at the Fort Worth Country Club. David Anderson, president of United Pharmaceuticals, calls at 1:30. He states he needs to speak with Ms. Winwright immediately. Write your response, providing all necessary details.

Situation 2

At 2:30 p.m., Ms. Winwright leaves for a meeting in David Anderson's office. She states that she does not know exactly when she will be back. Maurice P. Templeton, senior vice president and general counsel, calls and asks to see her at 8 a.m. the following morning. He says the meeting is urgent, and it will take approximately 30 minutes. He informs you that he cannot meet after 8:30 a.m. You notice Ms. Winwright already has a meeting scheduled on her calendar. However, you know she will not want to miss the 8 a.m. meeting with Mr. Templeton. Write your response.

Situation 3

At 3 p.m., a man calls for Ms. Winwright. He refuses to give his name or the purpose of his call. He states that he must talk with her. Ms. Winwright has not returned from her meeting with David Anderson. Write your response.

Situation 4

At 3:30 p.m. a reporter from the local newspaper calls and asks to speak to Ms. Winwright. (She has not returned from her meeting with David Anderson. She also has a 4 p.m. meeting scheduled.) The reporter tells you he is working on a story about a drug being developed by United Pharmaceuticals. The story will be published in tomorrow morning's newspaper. Write your response.

Situation 5

At 4 p.m. Ms. Winwright is in a conference call with two managers who report to her. Before going into the meeting, she asked that she not be disturbed. She told you the meeting would last approximately an hour and a half. At 4:30 p.m. Alexander Espinosa, chairperson of the Fort Worth Arts Committee, of which Ms. Winwright is a member, calls and asks to speak to Ms. Winwright. Write your response.

Practicing Telephone Etiquette

DIRECTIONS: Choose a class member to work with. Call each other, recreating the five situations in the previous activity. One of you should be the caller; the other should be the administrative assistant. Then switch roles and replay each situation. Rate each other on voice quality and the handling of the situations by using the Telephone Rating Form on the next page. Individually prepare an action plan on how you can improve your voice quality and/or techniques. Submit your action plan to your instructor.

TELEPHONE RATING FORM

Evaluate your team member's telephone techniques by checking *Yes* or *No* next to each of the statements below. Also evaluate the other person's handling of each situation and make notes for improvement if needed. Once you have evaluated each other on the rating form, prepare an action plan on how you can improve your telephone voice or technique. Give your action plan to your instructor.

Team Member's Name: _____

Quality Evaluated	Yes	No
1. The tone of voice used sounded friendly.		
2. The rate of speed was good—neither too fast nor too slow.		
3. The voice quality was varied. The person did not speak in a monotone.		
4. Each word was spoken clearly and was easily understood.		
5. The volume was at the right level—neither too high nor too low.		

Situation 1
Improvement needed:

Situation 2
Improvement needed:

Situation 3
Improvement needed:

Situation 4
Improvement needed:

Situation 5
Improvement needed:

Assessment of Learning Goals

DIRECTIONS: Review the Chapter 12 goals listed here. Did you successfully complete these goals? Evaluate yourself by completing the form below. If you did not satisfy the goal, state your reason(s) for not doing so.

1. Define *telecommunications* and describe the most common telecommunications pipelines and devices.

    Yes_____   No_____

2. Understand and use proper telephone etiquette.

    Yes_____   No_____

3. Identify telecommunications messaging services and the etiquette associated with their use.

    Yes_____   No_____

Chapter 13   Managing Paper and Electronic Records

English and Word Usage Drill

DIRECTIONS: Review the Punctuation Rules for the question mark, the exclamation point, and the dash in the Reference Guide of your textbook. Then correct the sentences below. Some sentences may be correct as written. Cite the rule that applies.

1. Stop playing with fire.

    Rule

2. Get to the bank early do not wait until the last minute.

    Rule

3. What day is best for our meeting. Tuesday. Wednesday.

    Rule

4. Answer your telephone promptly—between the first and second rings.

    Rule

5. No. I don't believe it.

    Rule

6. Should we schedule the test on Thursday.

   Rule

7. Call Mr. Bronson—he's vice president of customer relations—and ask for assistance.

   Rule

8. When will you finish your coursework and graduate from college.

   Rule

9. Emphasis on e-learning learning that takes place online is increasing throughout the nation.

   Rule

10. Will you please send the letter by express mail.

    Rule

Case Study: Organizing Paper Records

DIRECTIONS: Read the case below and answer the questions that follow the case.

CASE:

Dawon Abrego's work space is filled with stacks of papers. He has three neatly piled stacks on his desk and at least eight stacks on the floor. Although Dawon has two vertical filing cabinets, it appears most of the documents do not make it from the stacks to the cabinet. Many of Dawon's coworkers tease him about his unique filing system, but they are impressed that he can locate information in a short period of time. In fact, Dawon's system seems to work quite well for him. He has never had a problem locating information in a timely manner.

Two weeks ago Dawon requested an extended leave from work to take care of personal matters. In his absence, several projects were reassigned to other employees. The majority of these projects could not progress because the employees were unable to locate the necessary information in Dawon's stacks. One employee contacted Dawon, but Dawon could not guide him in locating the information. Although Dawon's supervisor did not approve of his filing methods, it was never an issue because Dawon was able to locate information in a timely manner. Now, however, the supervisor can see how Dawon's method has an impact on the workplace. Dawon will not be back in the office for at least three months.

QUESTIONS:

1. How can the supervisor handle this situation so the work gets done?

2. What suggestions could you make to the supervisor to prevent this type of problem from happening again?

Prepare Cross-References

DIRECTIONS:

1. Identify the indexing units in the business and personal names given below in the left column. Code the names by placing diagonals between the units, underlining the key unit, and numbering the remaining units.

2. In the right column, indicate how the names would be cross-referenced. Write the alternate name by which the record might be requested by the *X*. Write the name (in *as written* form) by *SEE* in the right column. Then code the name by *SEE*. If no cross-reference is required, write *No Cross-Reference Required* in the right column.

EXAMPLE:

2 3 4	X	2 3 4
Lawson / and / Maki / Meats		Maki / and / Lawson / Meats
		2 3 4
	SEE	Lawson / and / Maki / Meats

Filing Segment   **Cross-Reference (if needed)**

a.   WJPD Radio Station   X

                                         SEE

b.   Beck's is a popular name for   X

     Frazier Beck's Grill

                                         SEE

c.   Sideras and Shadduck Company   X

                                         SEE

d.   Reynolds-Flack Investment Firm   X

                                          SEE

e.   The Riverside Terrace   X

                                          SEE

f.   Joan M. Beckman-Phillips   X

                                          SEE

g.   South East Book Distributors   X

                                          SEE

h.   Mauruka's Diner   X

                                          SEE

i.   Smith, Childers, & Jones Inc.   X

                                          SEE

Organize Records for Subject Filing

Your supervisor, Melody Hoover, has gathered a large number of articles related to telecommunications. Melody has asked for your help in organizing the documents.

DIRECTIONS:

1. Organize the documents listed at the end of the exercise by subject. In a word processing document, key the following captions for main sections of the file: **COMMUNICATIONS**, **MANAGEMENT**, and **TELECOMMUNICATIONS**. Key the name of each document under the appropriate caption where it should be filed.

2. After you classify each document under one of the three major sections, examine the items under COMMUNICATIONS and divide this section into two subsections with the captions **CORRESPONDENCE** and **TELEPHONE**. Place the document names in the appropriate subsections of the file.

3. Repeat this process for each of the remaining two major subject classifications. Choose subheading captions that you think are appropriate.

4. Now organize the filing sections, subsections, and filenames in correct alphabetic order. Place the main section captions in order first. Within each main section, place the subsection captions in order. Then place the document names in each subsection in order.

DOCUMENT NAMES:
Increasing Cable Modem Speed
Management Training for the Future
Direct Dialing Can Save Money
How to Use Personality Tests
Using Analog Dial-Up
Bad Letters Do Not Get Results
How Good Is Your Telephone Voice?
Using VoIP to Increase Business
How to Set Up an International Call
Your Voice Speaks for the Company
Tests that Measure Office Productivity
Seminars that Work
Effective Satellite Connections
Tests Are a Management Tool
Do Short Workshops Succeed?
Writing Letters that Win Business
Increasing Your PDA Potential
The Top Ten Internet Connections
Is Your Phone Smarter Than You?
Answer with a Smile
Letters that Pay Off

Organize Record Numbers for Numeric Filing

DIRECTIONS:

1. The numbers below are record numbers that have been assigned to patients in a medical office. In a word processing file, key the numbers in sequence for consecutive numeric filing.

2. Key the numbers in sequence for terminal digit numeric filing.

3. Key the numbers in sequence in middle digit numeric filing.

190	69	229
998	66	890
190	44	190
552	66	154
348	23	199
998	34	223
348	23	234
029	36	229
248	48	103
128	28	001
442	20	890
906	75	229
442	20	115
998	66	234
629	29	393

Create a Database Query and Report

You work in the Records Management Department at ABC Corporation. ABC Corporation maintains an employee database that includes contact information for all employees. Your supervisor, Kyle Johannes, has asked that you prepare a list of employee names and phone numbers for all employees in the Records Management Department.

DIRECTIONS:

1. Open the *Access*™ database file *CH13 ABC Corp 2000* (if you have *Access 2003* or lower) or the file *CH13 ABC Corp 2007* (if you have *Access 2007)* found on the student CD. Prepare a query based on the Contact Data table. Name the query **Records Management Employees**. The query results should show:

   - Records for employees with *Records Management* in the Department field
   - The Employee ID, Last Name, First Name, and Phone fields

2. Create a report based on the Records Management Employees query. Include all fields in the report. Sort the records in ascending alphabetical order by last name and then by first name. Choose an attractive format that makes it easy to read all the data on the report. Select a report style that displays the report title at the top of the page. Name the report **Records Management Employees**. Print the report.

Assessment of Learning Goals

DIRECTIONS: Review the Chapter 13 goals listed here. Did you successfully complete these goals? Evaluate yourself by completing the form below. If you did not satisfy the goal, state your reason(s) for not doing so.

1. Understand the importance of records management.

   Yes_____   No_____

2. Describe the considerations in managing paper records.

   Yes_____   No_____

3. Describe the considerations in managing electronic records.

   Yes_____   No_____

4. Identify the factors associated with records retention, transfer, and disposal.

   Yes_____   No_____

Chapter 14   Personal Finance and Investment Strategies

English and Word Usage Drill

DIRECTIONS: Review the Punctuation Rules for quotation marks, omission marks or ellipsis, and parentheses in the Reference Guide to your textbook. Then correct the sentences below. Some sentences may be correct as written. Cite the rule that applies.

1. Rebecca said, "I will be seeking a bachelor's degree at our local university when I complete my internship in France".

    Rule

2. The author of the book states, I have found that most people are not aware of how much in interest charges they pay when they only pay a portion of their credit card debt.

    Rule

3. The instructor announced, "There will be a test over this material tomorrow".

    Rule

4. I recently read an article entitled, The Smart Investor.

    Rule

5. I found these quotes interesting that are taken from the article, The Smartest Investment Book You'll Ever Read:"

    Remember this general rule: the larger the percentage of stock in your portfolio the greater the risk. It is also important to appreciate the differences in the upside and downside potential of a very conservative and a very risky portfolio.

    For example, for the thirty-five year period ending in 2004, a very conservative portfolio consisting entirely of intermediate-term government bonds would have had an annualized return of 8.5 percent.

    Rule

6. The following is a partial quote from his presentation, "Save, save, and save! If you adopt this approach, you will be surprised at how much your savings will grow. Few people who follow this advice ever find themselves without resources to   "

   Rule

7. The house was beyond their means since it cost five hundred thousand dollars $500,000.

   Rule

8. The number of people in the Accounting Department including the most recent hires is now 35.

   Rule

9. The AMA American Management Association is planning a meeting on investment strategies.

   Rule

10. The three reasons given for the decrease in sales of the office furniture were: 1 the product was not advertised effectively, 2 the furniture was priced out of the reach of the small businessperson, and 3 the economy is slow at the present and businesses are not replacing their used furniture.

    Rule

Case Study: Investing Options

DIRECTIONS: Read the case below and respond to the questions.

CASE:

One of your friends comes to you with this story:

I am considering putting 10 percent of my weekly paycheck into investments. I have never invested before. I bought an investment book and read all of it. However, I still do not feel comfortable with the idea of investing. I know the difference between stocks and bonds, but I really do not understand mutual funds. I am intrigued by the stock market but do not know what I should consider before purchasing a stock. Help! What should I do?

QUESTIONS:

1. What advice do you give your friend regarding how to learn more about investing?

2. How can a person who knows little about stocks and bonds own investments that are diversified and professionally managed?

Risk Tolerance Quiz

DIRECTIONS: Answer the following questions on your own and then discuss your answers with one of your classmates. Compare how you have answered the questions. Did you answer them similarly? How would you classify yourself based on your answers? Are you a risk taker with money or are you extremely cautious?

1. Which of the following statements describes you?

    a. I carefully consider each dollar I spend.
    b. If I want something, I buy it; it does not matter what the cost is.
    c. If I do not have the cash money for a purchase (even though I want an item), I do not buy it.

2. You are on a TV game show where you have a chance to make money. Here is where you are in the game you are playing: You have the option of taking the $500 or attempting to answer the next question, which is worth $500 more dollars. If you fail to answer the question, you will lose the $500 you already have. What would you do?

    a. Take the chance
    b. Walk away

3. How comfortable are you with investing in stocks?

    a. I would invest in stocks if I had the money.
    b. I would never invest in stocks; it is too risky.

4. Do you consider yourself a saver or a spender?

    a. A saver
    b. A spender

5. What does the word "risk" mean to you?

    a. There is a chance for failure.
    b. There is a chance for success.

6. Suppose a relative left you an inheritance of $200,000. Which of the following choices would you make?

    a. I would immediately put the money in savings.
    b. I would invest the money in stocks and bonds.

7. If you were consulting with a broker and she or he asked you what type of investment strategies you would use of the following, what would your answer be?

    a. Low-risk investments
    b. Medium-risk investments
    c. High-risk investments

8. You have been saving for two years for a vacation in Europe; you have saved $7,500 and you already have your reservations for your dream trip. You were told yesterday that your job with the company will end in two months (due to financial issues with the company—not your performance). What would you do?

    a. Take the trip; I have saved for it and I deserve. I can find a job later.
    b. Cancel the trip; I need to find a job. My financial security comes before a European trip.

9. A relative left you $100,000. How would you use the money?

    a. Take off a year from work and travel.
    b. Immediately put the money in a mutual fund account.
    c. Put the money in a savings account where you can earn 5 percent interest.

10. When you think of the word *risk*, what comes to your mind first?

    a. Uncertainty
    b. Opportunity

Stocks Research

DIRECTIONS:

1. Select two Fortune 500 companies. You can find a list of Fortune 500 companies by searching the Internet using the search term *Fortune 500 companies*.

2. For each company, investigate the company to learn:
   - The business of the company—the industry sector and the products or services the company produces or provides
   - The company history—when the company began and its growth
   - The company's present financial condition

3. Track the stock price for each company for two weeks.

4. From what you have learned about the companies, determine whether or not you think each stock would be a good investment at the present time. Explain why or why not for each stock in a memo to your instructor. Use the *Word* file *Memo Form* to create the memo.

Assessment of Chapter Goals

DIRECTIONS: Review the Chapter 14 goals listed here. Did you successfully complete these goals? Evaluate yourself by completing the form below. If you did not satisfy the goal, state your reason(s) for not doing so.

1. Identify mandatory and optional payroll deductions.

   Yes_____   No_____

2. Analyze organizational financial statements.

   Yes_____   No_____

3. Discuss traditional and online banking functions.

   Yes_____   No_____

4. Identify options for personal investments.

   Yes_____   No_____

Chapter 15   Event Planning

English and Word Usage Drill

DIRECTIONS: Review the Subject and Verb Agreement section in the Reference Guide of your textbook. Then correct the sentences below. Some sentences may be correct as written. Cite the rule that applies.

1.   Either the delegates or the vice president are going to handle registration during the convention.

   Rule

2.   The number of requests for wireless network access are increasing every year.

   Rule

3.   One of the administrative assistants want to take a computer course next semester.

   Rule

4.   Every participant in the competition is going to receive a ribbon.

   Rule

5.   Not only the managers but also the salespeople has access to the latest marketing information.

   Rule

6. Few members was willing to voice their opinions to the committee chair.

   Rule

7. A number of committee members was willing to stay late and clean up after the meeting.

   Rule

8. Emily or Connor will pick up the mail tomorrow.

   Rule

9. Something was wrong with the copy machine last week.

   Rule

10. The Hawaiian Islands are the site for the convention next year.

    Rule

Case Study: Meeting Planning

DIRECTIONS: Read the case below and answer the questions that follow the case. Discuss this case with three of your classmates. As a group, prepare a memo to your instructor that includes a summary of your responses.

CASE:

Francine Higgins has been working at United Pharmaceuticals for six months. On several occasions, Francine was asked to set up meetings for three or four people within the company. Francine merely called the employees and gave them the date, time, and location for the meetings. The attendees usually met in an open office or conference room. No one asked Francine to do anything else.

Last week Francine's employer, Kyle Rathman, asked her to set up a meeting for five executives from Reinhart's Medical Supplies and three executives at United Pharmaceuticals. Although planning a meeting this large was new to Francine, she used her calendaring software to arrange the meeting with the executives in the company, and she called those executives outside the firm. She gave them the date, time, and location of the meeting over the phone.

When it was time for the meeting to begin, the group was unable to find the meeting room. Mr. Rathman had to find Francine (who was on her morning break) to learn why a conference room was not reserved. Francine quickly found an empty conference room on another floor and went back on break. Soon Mr. Rathman was looking for Francine again because he could not locate the equipment for showing a video. Francine called the Media Department to request the equipment; it was delivered in 20 minutes. Mr. Rathman convened the meeting and Francine returned to her desk. Mr. Rathman called a few minutes later asking Francine when she would be joining the meeting to record the minutes.

At the conclusion of the meeting, Francine transcribed the proceedings and gave them to Mr. Rathman. When he asked Francine if copies had been sent to the other attendees, Francine said they had not. Mr. Rathman became very upset. He accused Francine of lacking professionalism and not understanding the negative impression people get by attending an improperly planned meeting. As he left the office, Mr. Rathman turned and told Francine that she had not even had the foresight to order coffee for his guests.

QUESTIONS:

1. What steps should Francine have taken in planning the meeting?

2. How might Francine have helped Mr. Rathman make a more professional appearance to the attendees?

3. Does Mr. Rathman have any responsibility for the poor meeting. If so, what are his responsibilities?

4. What should Francine's reactions to Mr. Rathman's comments be?

Making Meeting Arrangements

DIRECTIONS: Your supervisor, Melody Hoover, is the chair of a research task force that includes individuals from United Pharmaceuticals and other local organizations. She has asked you to set up a research task force meeting.

1. Schedule the meeting for the second Wednesday of next month. There will be ten individuals in attendance. She has provided you with the following information.
   - The meeting room should be available from 9:00 a.m. until 3:30 p.m.
   - The meeting should start with a continental breakfast from 9:00 a.m. until 9:30 a.m.
   - A computer display projector and screen will be needed.
   - A whiteboard or flipchart for taking notes will be required.
   - Lunch will be provided for all participants.

2. Research at least two conference centers or hotels in your area that can accommodate this meeting.

3. Prepare a spreadsheet that includes the individual and total cost estimates for each venue. Make sure your cost estimates are complete.

4. Prepare a memorandum that describes each option and include your recommendation to Melody. Use the *Word* file *Memo Form* to prepare the memo. Attach the spreadsheet to the memo.

Preparing Meeting Materials

DIRECTIONS: Melody has decided to follow your recommendation for her research task force meeting next month. In preparation for that meeting, she has asked that you prepare a meeting notice, an agenda, and an evaluation form for the meeting. The purpose of the meeting is to implement several quality measures for the research committee. The objectives of the meeting are to discuss the creation of a Quality Control Board and to present information from the Annual Research Conference.

1. Use the information gathered in the previous activity to create a meeting notice.

2. Use the suggestions given in the textbook to prepare and format a meeting agenda. Melody has provided you with the following information to be included on the agenda.

   - The meeting will start at 9:30 a.m.; the continental breakfast should be scheduled from 9:00 to 9:30 a.m.
   - Melody will need about 10 minutes at the beginning of the meeting to introduce the individuals in attendance.
   - Leonardo Richie will outline how to be an effective board member from 9:40 a.m. until 10:25 a.m.
   - There will be a 15-minute break starting at 10:25 a.m.
   - Leslie Beckman will lead the discussion of the creation of a Quality Control Board from 10:40 a.m. until 11:40 a.m.
   - Lunch will be served from noon until 1:15 p.m. Allow participants a few minutes to freshen up before lunch.
   - Bruce Walton will review information from the Annual Research Conference from 1:15 p.m. until 2:00 p.m.
   - Elizabeth Jenkins will introduce a Review Board assessment instrument from 2:00 p.m. until 2:40 p.m.
   - Melody Hoover will answer questions and wrap up the meeting from 2:40 p.m. until 3:00 p.m.

3. Create an effective meeting evaluation form that Melody can distribute at the end of the meeting.

Assessment of Learning Goals

DIRECTIONS: Review the Chapter 15 goals listed here. Did you successfully complete these goals? Evaluate yourself by completing the form below. If you did not satisfy the goal, state your reason(s) for not doing so.

1. Describe the characteristics of effective meetings and the wide variety of meeting formats.

   Yes_____   No_____

2. Describe the roles and responsibilities of individuals associated with a meeting.

   Yes_____   No_____

3. Plan meetings and prepare materials related to meetings.

   Yes_____   No_____

4. Participate in effective meetings and evaluate meetings.

   Yes_____   No_____

Chapter 16   Travel Arrangements

English and Word Usage Drill

DIRECTIONS: Review the Punctuation Rules for Pronouns in the Reference Guide of your textbook. Then correct the sentences below. Some sentences may be correct as written. Cite the rule that applies.

1. You're attention to detail made the project a success.

    Rule

2. Whom shall I say is calling?

    Rule

3. Roxanne said she will give the opening address at the convention.

    Rule

4. She is the only vice president that does not have a company car.

    Rule

5. He found himself the only one in favor of the proposal.

    Rule

6. The neighbors invited my husband and I to a barbeque this weekend.

   Rule

7. Elizabeth and Edward are working hard on his and her projects for the science fair.

   Rule

8. Estelle's report on ergonomics, that I sent you last week, will be helpful when arranging your office furniture.

   Rule

9. The person whom I recommended for the job does not have a degree in business.

   Rule

10. Neither Ingrid nor Rachel wants to do their share.

   Rule

Case Study: International Travel

DIRECTIONS: Read the case below and answer the questions that follow the case.

CASE:

One of your friends from the local chapter of IAAP, Kimberly Lockhart, is going to visit India for two weeks. She knows United Pharmaceuticals has an office in India. Kim also knows you have met executives from the New Delhi office through your job at United Pharmaceuticals and that you work with an administrative assistant who is a native of New Delhi. She has never traveled outside the United States and has not done any research on people of other cultures. She asks you for advice on how she should prepare for the trip.

QUESTIONS:

1. How can you help Kimberly prepare for her trip?

2. How can Kimberly prepare so that she understands the culture and customs of the people of New Delhi?

Flyer on Airline Safety

DIRECTIONS:

Your supervisor has asked you to prepare a flyer that gives tips for airline safety.

1. Create a one-page flyer to distribute to all employees that includes five tips for airline safety. The flyer should also contain a listing of several items that are prohibited on airplanes.

2. Format the flyer attractively. Include a title, a bulleted list, and graphics.

3. Print the flyer.

Name _____

Assessment of Learning Goals

DIRECTIONS: Review the Chapter 16 goals listed here. Did you successfully complete these goals? Evaluate yourself by completing the form below. If you did not satisfy the goal, state your reason(s) for not doing so.

1. Effectively make domestic and international travel arrangements.

   Yes_____   No_____

2. Research business customs related to international travel.

   Yes_____   No_____

3. Implement organizational travel procedures.

   Yes_____   No_____

Chapter 17   Job Search and Advancement

English and Word Usage Drill

DIRECTIONS: Review the Spelling Rules in the Reference Guide to your textbook. Then correct the sentences below. Some sentences may be correct as written. Cite the rule that applies.

1. I did not recieve the telegram in time to respond.

    Rule

2. The books wieghed ten pounds.

    Rule

3. When I droped the bag in the yard, I broke three bottles of perfume.

    Rule

4. I concured with the decision to wait until Saturday morning to start the trip to China.

    Rule

5. He actted as if I was not in the room.

    Rule

6. I was warmlly received by all the members of the group.

Rule

7. The product was not useable after it had been in the sun for two hours.

Rule

8. I clued the young man as to the type of music that was played at the symphony.

Rule

9. The group travelled to Japan.

Rule

10. I lost the arguement, but I did not let myself be concerned abou the outcome.

Rule

Practice Interview Questions

DIRECTIONS: Key answers to the following questions that you might be asked in an interview. Share your answers with a classmate and ask for constructive feedback.

1. What are your career goals?

2. What are your strengths related to your career?

3. What are your weaknesses related to your career??

4. How confident are you that you can successfully perform the duties of this position?

5. Do you consider yourself creative? If so, give a sample of a creative solution to a problem.

6. How do you respond to stress?

7. What is the greatest risk that you have ever taken?

8. Have you ever failed at something? If so, how did you handle it?

9. In what type of atmosphere do you work best?

10. Why did you leave (or do you want to leave) your previous (current) job?

Interview a Supervisor

DIRECTIONS:

1. Interview a supervisor of a local business. The interview may be in person or by phone or email. Ask the person the questions listed below.

2. Prepare a written summary of the interview. Be prepared to present your summary to the class.

QUESTIONS:

- In your experience, what contributes to employees losing their jobs?

- Do individuals lose their jobs more often due to lack of job knowledge and performance skills (computer skills, composition skills, and so on) or lack of skills in communication, human relations, critical thinking, time management, and decision making?

- Does your company have a formal evaluation plan for all employees? If so, how often does evaluation occur? If no formal evaluation plan exists, how are employees evaluated?

- What growth opportunities does your organization provide employees?

Assessment of Chapter Goals

DIRECTIONS: Review the Chapter 17 goals listed here. Did you successfully complete these goals? Evaluate yourself by completing the form below. If you did not satisfy the goal, state your reason(s) for not doing so.

1. Understand your skills, interests, and abilities as they relate to a career.

    Yes_____   No_____

2. Determine a job search plan.

    Yes_____   No_____

3. Identify sources of job information and research organizations of interest.

    Yes_____   No_____

4. Prepare a resume and letter of application.

    Yes_____   No_____

5. Demonstrate effective interview skills.

    Yes_____   No_____

6. Develop job advancement strategies.

    Yes_____   No_____

Chapter 18   Leadership and Management: Challenges and Characteristics

English and Word Usage Drill

DIRECTIONS: Review the Spelling Rules in the Reference Guide of your textbook. Then correct the sentences below in the space provided. Some sentences may be correct as written. Cite the rule that applies.

1. I felt strongly that the new employee was lying to me.

   Rule

2. The workload was not a managable one.

   Rule

3. I thought the new administrative assistant was lieing to me concerning her skills.

   Rule

4. The trafficing of drugs across the border has become a major problem.

   Rule

5. I felt extremely lonely; however, my friend felt even lonelyer.

   Rule

6. The girl appeared to be heavyier than the last time I saw her.

    Rule

7. I did not buy the potatos in the market; they were too large for baking.

    Rule

8. The children were enjoying riding the donkeys.

    Rule

9. I went back to buy the two kittys I had admired at the pet store; however, they had already been sold when I returned to the store.

    Rule

10. The two afternoon trollies run at 2 p.m. and 4 p.m.

    Rule

Case Study: Hiring an Administrative Assistant

DIRECTIONS: Read the case below and respond to the questions and instructions that follow the case.

CASE:

You have been with United Pharmaceuticals for one year. Melody Hoover and Amando Hinojosa have continued to give you more responsibility. You have been able to increase your skills tremendously during your time at United. You will be graduating within the next month; you plan to apply for positions in another state. You have given a month's notice to both Melody and Amando.

Melody has asked if you would be interested in interviewing the four part-time assistants that have applied for your position. You feel honored that she respects your opinion, and you want to do a good job. She has asked that you develop a list of questions that you will ask the individuals and submit the questions to her for review.

You have now interviewed the four applicants; you do not feel that any of them are qualified to do the job. You tell Melody that you believe the job search should be extended since none of the candidates seem to have the skills needed to do the work. You were not involved in the initial vacancy notice preparation. You think that another vacancy notice should be developed and the job advertised again.

QUESTIONS:

1. What questions will you ask the individuals at the interview? Key a list of the questions.

2. What information should be included in the job vacancy notice? Write an appropriate job vacancy notice for the position.

Evaluate Leadership Skills

DIRECTIONS: Evaluate your leadership understanding and effectiveness by keying responses to the items below. There are no correct or incorrect responses to items. Your task is to honestly evaluate your leadership skills and determine ways in which you may improve your skills.

1. I believe that an effective leader has these characteristics:

2. My leadership traits include the following:

3. In order to be a more effective leader, I need to work on the following areas of weakness:

Professional Growth Plan

DIRECTIONS:

1. In Chapter 1 you were asked to:
   - Identify specific goals that you want to achieve, listing the goals and a completion date.
   - Identify at least three goals that you plan to achieve this semester.
   - Make a list of all the skills that you think you have, such as keyboarding, computer (listing the various computer competencies that you have), human relations skills, and so forth.
   - Complete a self-evaluation chart and discuss your evaluation with a trusted friend, coworker, or family member.
   - Determine areas of growth that you need to focus on in this course and develop a list of growth objectives that you want to accomplish.

2. Retrieve the list of goals, the skills list, the self-evaluation chart, and the list of growth objectives you completed in Chapter 1. Identify the goals you have achieved and those you have yet to achieve.

3. Complete column 2 of the self-evaluation chart from Chapter 1. Compare your responses to those you entered earlier. How have your responses changed?

4. Examine your list of growth objectives. Identify the objectives you have achieved and those you have yet to achieve. Continue to work on your growth objectives as you continue your education and enter the business world as an employee.

5. In Chapter 1 you began collecting files of your work to place in an e-portfolio. In Chapter 13 you organized the files you had created thus far into folders according to the skills demonstrated. You also renamed the files using a system that describes the content of the file. Review your e-portfolio once again. Add updated copies of your professional goals and growth objectives. Continue to add files to your e-portfolio as you develop new skills in other courses or on the job.

Assessment of Chapter Goals

DIRECTIONS: Review the Chapter 18 goals listed here. Did you successfully complete these goals? Evaluate yourself by completing the form below. If you did not satisfy the goal, state your reason(s) for not doing so.

1. Define *leadership* and describe leadership traits.

   Yes_____   No_____

2. Define *management* and describe the functions of management.

   Yes_____   No_____

3. Determine the administrative professional's job responsibilities.

   Yes_____   No_____

4. Discuss the benefits of a healthy lifestyle, including proper diet and physical exercise.

   Yes_____   No_____